M000086741

disORDER

disORDER

Phil Hamman

eLectio Publishing

Little Elm, TX

www.eLectioPublishing.com

Bonnie &
John,
God's Peace be
with you.
Phil
Hamman
8-16-15

disORDER

By Phil Hamman

Copyright 2014 by Phil Hamman

Cover Design by eLectio Publishing

ISBN-13: 978-1-63213-061-7

Published by eLectio Publishing, LLC

Little Elm, Texas

http://www.eLectioPublishing.com

Printed in the United States of America

Scriptures taken from the Holy Bible, New International Version®, NIV®. Copyright © 1973, 1978, 1984, 2011 by Biblica, Inc.™ Used by permission of Zondervan. All rights reserved worldwide.www.zondervan.com The "NIV" and "New International Version" are trademarks registered in the United States Patent and Trademark Office by Biblica, Inc.™

Without limiting the rights under copyright reserved above, no part of this publication may be reproduced, stored in or introduced into a retrieval system, or transmitted, in any form, or by any means (electronic, mechanical, photocopying, recording, or otherwise), without the prior written permission of both the copyright owner and the above publisher of this book.

If you purchased this book without a cover, you should be aware that this book is stolen property. It was reported as "unsold and destroyed" to the publisher and neither the author nor the publisher has received any payment for the "stripped book."

The scanning, uploading, and distribution of this book via the Internet or via any other means without the permission of the publisher is illegal and punishable by law. Please purchase only authorized electronic editions, and do not participate in or encourage electronic piracy of copyrighted materials. Your support of the author's rights is appreciated.

Publisher's Note

The publisher does not have any control over and does not assume any responsibility for author or third-party websites or their content.

CONTENTS

PART THREE: THE LIGHTED ROADS

Acknowledgments

My sincere thanks to:

Sandy, my exceptional wife, for her patience and love while I went through many changes to overcome past demons, and for all her support and help while writing this memoir. My children, Jordan and Angela, for their love and for blessing my world each and every day. Wanda Wulff-Dickson, Jeff Maschino, and Irv Moeller, who all lived the life in the Norton-Froehlich area and shared their experiences. My co-teacher in English IV, Michelle Pick, for her extremely helpful editing suggestions. My neighbor Terry Lane, a retired college English and German professor, for his sense of humor and input. My special teachers and coaches whom I tell about in this book. You taught me what commitment means and how to go about setting and achieving goals. All of my friends, including Matt Lofton and Doug Wallin, who are like family to me; Leonard Sorenson, Curt Ager, Wilbur, Chuck Kruger, and Jim Anderson, who made it through the dark times with me. I wish you all the best. My life is better for having you all as friends. Steve Joslyn for always being there through the bad and the good. The eLectio team, especially Jesse and Christopher, for their tireless work in building a professional, ethical publishing company.

Benny, David, and the teens I knew growing up who died way too young, rest in peace.

Prologue

When my first book, *Under the Influence,* took off, I was humbly stunned. What had started as a simple story of my life for my children had led me down an unexpected road. I was soon speaking before an audience nearly every week and sharing this story of the many twists and turns in the path I took to overcome an impoverished neighborhood and many other obstacles I faced. So, when I began writing *disORDER,* I wrote it in such a way that my two books can be read in either sequence or independently.

When condensing five decades of one's life, clearly many events cannot be included. Although I don't remember the exact words of every conversation, I have written all events to the best of my memory. On most stories, I also collaborated with at least one other person who was involved in the events. I used people's real names except for "Freddy," which is a pseudonym. To connect related events, I don't always write in chronological order. I carefully considered the truth of each story, asked for the perspectives of others involved where I could, and even bared my own mistakes, immature thinking, and illegal, sometimes violent, decisions. It is my desire that when people read about themselves, they will at least feel that I have told about events as accurately and truthfully as humanly possible. Some situations are harsh, but they are the facts of what occurred, and I was as fair as I felt I rightfully could be.

Finally, I hope that people who read this book, especially teachers or those who work with our youth, will feel they have a better understanding of the effects of poverty on life decisions as well as the heartbreaking challenges faced by many children around the nation on a daily basis.

Scrapper

"Top of the World" by the Carpenters pounded from the radio, echoing my disposition. I had my windows rolled down and the warm May air blew a feeling of déjà vu through the cab of my Blazer. I was returning from the post office, where I had just mailed a package to an old college buddy who was living in Texas. Driving past the elementary school near my home, I noticed three boys in the open grassy field next to the school building. The school day was long over, and it was obvious from their aggressive stances that these boys were not playing. This was a fight. It appeared that the two older boys were beating up the smaller boy.

My foot automatically jumped to the brake, and I slowly turned the corner toward the school parking lot. I watched this fight in progress as I rolled to a stop. The little guy kept getting flung to the ground yet popped right back up, charging his two foes, only to find himself sprawled on the grass again. The little guy looked to be about eight years old and all of sixty pounds. The others were at least two years older and packing more weight—an outnumbered mismatch of a brawl. I exited my vehicle and slammed the door, although this failed to capture their attention. Something about the situation pulled at my stomach as I advanced toward the fracas thirty yards away. The little guy had just received a solid punch to the side of his head and down on his knees he went. In a second, he was back on his feet swinging his fists and spewing a torrent of swear words that echoed across the playground. Memories flooded back. I had to admire this little scrapper. He had grit.

"Hey! What's going on here?" I yelled, stepping right in between the boys. Wide-eyed and caught off-guard, the two bigger boys stopped cold, but the little scrapper tried to come barreling right through me, fire in his eyes, in an effort to get to the bigger bullies.

"Whoa, whoa! Hold on, buddy," I said to the scrapper gently, holding him back while his feet kicked wildly at the two boys who now stood silent and sheepish.

His lip was bloody, and a small knot was forming under his left eye. He stood, fists clenched, teeth gritted, and shaking in anger. I waved the bigger boys away.

"You two! Beat it and head for home!" I ordered.

When they were gone, the little guy broke down sobbing.

"They pick on me all the time!" he choked out between convulsive sobs.

"Hey, you did fine. Don't worry about it. You stood up for yourself," I assured him. "Try to avoid those guys and go home. Get yourself cleaned up."

I stood there until the little guy was completely out of sight. When I got back to my vehicle, I sat in that parking lot for a long time. The little scrapper had brought back a flood of memories. I drifted back in time to my younger days. Back to a time of bloody challenges and senseless brawls born from anger, frustration, and misery. My mind raced back to the streets of Norton-Froehlich.

PART ONE

THE

DARK

ROADS

Matthew 7:13-14

"*Enter through the narrow gate. For wide is the gate and broad is the road that leads to destruction, and many enter through it.*"

Bullies, Beatings, and Big Rings

Every morning before school, I walked two blocks to a crossroad where the school bus ran a loop through the Norton section, which was the area of town where I lived. On my pickup corner, there were anywhere from six to twelve kids on a given morning. I was talking with one of my classmates when…

Snap!

"Ouch!" I cried out. I looked left and right, thinking a hornet had stung me on the back of the neck. When I turned, I saw Patrick, one of the older kids from the neighborhood, laughing. He stood with a sneer, deviously waving a snapper back and forth in front of my face. A snapper was made from a metal bobby pin that was bent and curled into a spring-loaded device that could be cocked and loaded to inflict pain on an unsuspecting victim. I took a step back and watched him move on to new prey. He pressed the curled end against another kid's neck and released it with a devastating snap, leaving that kid howling in pain and rubbing at the angry red welt rising from his neck.

I casually moved away from Patrick and blended into the middle of a large group of kids who were all waiting for our school bus to show up. Sometimes the harassment turned into a fistfight, but this kid was older and bigger. I was not going to punch him. Patrick was just one of the bullies who operated in Norton-Froehlich.

Riding the bus was a lesson in learning to avoid pain and suffering while getting from the bus stop to school. The older kids and bullies had all kinds of devious tricks to torture others and didn't hesitate to use sharp pencils, needles, or anything else that inflicted pain. Sometimes kids walked off the bus with a huge glob of green spit in their hair. Several times I was punched in the stomach so hard it really did knock the wind out of me. I'd double over, gasping for air. Some of these boys wore up to three big rings on each hand. They'd

9

rotate the rings so the gaudy part was face down and then slap someone on top of the head.

The rings were also used like brass knuckles in a fistfight. There had been a lot of talk about an argument building up to a fight after school between two of the older, tougher kids from my neighborhood. It started when one of them pinched the other guy's girlfriend on the butt. After a heated discussion on the bus, they decided to fight in a vacant lot, so most of us stayed on the bus until we reached that spot, eagerly piling out of the bus to watch the action. They squared off in the field and started throwing jabs like two boxers. They both landed some good punches on the other person's face with the hard knobs of their rings. After about forty seconds, one got the other by the hair and punched him repeatedly in the face. The butt-pincher was on top and eventually won when the other kid yelled, "That's enough!" When they got ready to part ways, the victor said, "See, I'll pinch your girlfriend's butt if I want." Both left with welts and cuts on their faces from the rings.

I was standing by my locker at Axtell Junior High when a ninth grader came by and kneed me as hard as he could, for no reason, in the upper thigh. I got a horrible charley horse. I tried to take a step but buckled onto the hallway floor. Not wanting to get caught in a vulnerable position, I got right back up and hobbled down the hall. I realized how devastatingly painful it was, so I started doing it too. It was an easy way to mess with someone. So I jumped on the bullying bandwagon myself.

In the showers after P.E., I, as did other kids, gave what we called stingers. A stinger is a slap with a flat hand on wet skin which caused a severe stinging sensation. The stinger left a perfect red hand print on the victim's back and left him shrieking in pain. Another mean pastime we enjoyed was tripping kids as they ran for the lunch line. There were a lot of students at Axtell Junior High, so if you ended up at the back of the line, your eating time was greatly reduced. Kids would sprint down the hall to get a front spot in line, and I would stand by the lockers and quickly stick my foot out on someone running by. The kid would fly through the air and slide on his stomach for several feet along the waxed floor. The victim's books, papers, and personal items would be strewn all along the hallway; then other mean guys would kick the books further down the hall, ensuring this humiliated kid would end up at the rear of the lunch line.

Girls weren't immune from our torment. Wanda Wulff was a junior high girl who was still adjusting to the unexpected death of her father. She was a harmless loner—not the scowling, greasy-haired type but a kind-hearted dreamer—who preferred fashion and teen magazines over textbooks because of their glossy-paged promises of a better life somewhere beyond the borders of South Dakota. On one particular day, my eye caught this random, distracted victim rushing toward the cafeteria with an armful of books and magazines. The timing was impeccable. My foot swept out in front of her, connecting at the perfect sweet spot that sent Wanda airborne, her outstretched arms throwing a spray of papers into the air. She landed with a thud and slid several feet on her stomach, her dress curling up dangerously close to what could have been an even more embarrassing moment. *Perfect.* I strolled on down the hall and Wanda, who suffered only a bruised ego, rose to her feet. Every attempt she made to reclaim a book or paper was thwarted by the throngs of students pressing by. Yet she managed to recover everything, all the while feeling the eyes of a thousand gawkers passing by with no offers to help her. I was just taking one last look back at the spectacle I'd created when a teacher grabbed me and yelled at me for what I had done.

"It was an accident," I explained, smirking. The teacher let me go on my way.

People might wonder why adults let this bullying happen. In reality, back then, many adults were more likely to tell us to stick up for ourselves and just deal with it. This happened to my friend Joe when he was in sixth grade and got on the bad side of a group of tough kids. He was walking home when they spotted him. Joe took off with the angry mob in hot pursuit. Joe was able to

11

slide through the door of a local store just as they closed in on him, and he ran to the owner.

"I need help! Those kids outside are going to beat me up!"

The owner shook his head back and forth and pointed to the door. "Hell no! You just go back outside and whatever happens to you, happens. You stole from here last month, so get outside!"

It was true. Joe had been caught shoplifting a candy bar a few weeks prior. His heart sunk as he realized he had to leave the safe haven and take his chances with the wolf pack pacing outside. Joe slowly walked to the door, hoping for a last-minute change of heart, then stepped outside where he took a serious beating. He went on to become a champion wrestler in high school and college, perhaps spurred on to become tougher due to his life experiences.

Jeff Maschino, a kid I went to school with, lived in the Froehlich section and had a rough time nearly every day after school. He had to look down each street, checking for bullies to decide a safe route to make it home without having something bad happen. Jeff still has a scar under his eye where a mean kid bashed him across the face with a bottle.

When I was in fourth grade, I also got caught out in an open field, like a sitting duck. Three kids came out of nowhere and surrounded me.

"Let's depants him!" one of them shouted.

A horrible picture formed in my mind of me walking down the street in just my underwear. I'd recently watched another boy, David, get depantsed by a group of kids who then hoisted his jeans to the top of the flagpole. David was a skinny little guy who did not live in Norton-Froehlich but got schooled fast and harsh when he came up to hang out with me. First, these bullies grabbed David in a choke hold and dragged him to a flagpole. One of them put the flag snap onto a belt loop of his blue jeans.

"We're going to run you up to the top of the flagpole!"

Once they got him snapped on, they pulled the cable pulley wire and David went skyward, but when he was up about eight feet, his belt loop broke, and he came tumbling back to earth. David was shaken up, but nothing was broken.

"Well, if we can't hoist him up, we'll put his pants up there." And they did.

David had to stand humiliated in his underwear until the bullies left, and then he was able to pull his pants back down from the top of the flagpole. I stood back and watched, just glad it wasn't me. I don't remember David ever coming back to our area to hang out after that flagpole stunt. Incidentally, David died from huffing when he was fourteen years old.

All of this raced through my mind as I stood determined not to go down without a fight. These kids were about my age, so I thought I had a fighting chance to keep my pants on. Before anyone could grab me, I went after one kid and punched him hard in the jaw, but the other two closed in on me and flung me to the ground. They pinned me down, and one kid unsnapped my jeans and started pulling them off. With all my strength, I twisted and kicked. One kid was at my feet, trying to pull the bottom of my pant leg, and one of my kicks finally caught him right in the nose. He inched back and gave up. I held onto my belt loops and continued squirming, kicking, and threatening to break their noses until they finally gave up and left me alone.

Some kids became experts at avoiding these bullies. But many times it seemed like I was where the action was when it came to these mean kids. Also, I was a little guy, so, of course, the bullies focused on me or any other smaller kids. We learned to depend on our wits and to find allies, especially older kids who could be called on to serve as occasional bodyguards. I was fortunate to find an older buddy in Irvin Moeller. His brother Donny, who ended up being executed, was someone I always feared in the neighborhood, but Irvin was someone I trusted. He came to my defense a few times. I owe him.

Tainted Love

To understand what brought me to this lifestyle of bullying, fistfighting, and danger, one must first understand my parents. In her younger years, my mom, Darlene, had beautiful fair skin, blue eyes, and auburn hair that she painstakingly curled to perfection every day. Her physical features came from her Irish heritage on her dad's side of the family. My mom adored her father, though she had only a few treasured memories of him before he committed suicide during the Great Depression when she was only six years old. He left behind his wife, Meta, and seven children with no means to support themselves. Meta's relatives were cruel and frequently came to the house threatening to take the seven children away from her. To protect her family, Meta ingrained the idea in her children that total dedication to the family was essential to keep them together. They were to help each other without question, protect the family name, and never, ever leave home. They needed each other. They needed to stay together, work together, and pool all their resources to survive. Everything they did was for "the family."

My mom, however, had a wide streak of Irish rebellion running through her veins. Even as a child, she was the difficult one. Food was scarce during the Depression, often leaving the family of eight with one chicken to share for the evening meal. Everyone's mouth watered the day a generous neighbor brought over a birthday cake topped with a meager dab of frosting spread thin to cover the entire dessert.

"I want *that* piece!" my mom squealed, pointing to the slice with the most frosting.

Not one to bow to a demanding child, Meta gave her a different piece, which my mom promptly threw to the floor with all the strength a six-year-old could muster. The cake burst into a smattering of crumbs, and my mom sat

15

fuming, arms crossed, head down, rather than eat the only piece of cake she'd be offered that year.

As the children in the family became old enough to work, they were expected to present their weekly earnings to Meta, who would decide how the money would be spent in order to, of course, benefit the entire family. My mom's first job was as a waitress at Kirk's Café in Sioux Falls, South Dakota. Kirk's was a popular fifties diner with vinyl booths and a glass pie case opposite the old-fashioned malt machine behind the counter. It was run by a Greek immigrant who over the years never failed to find a job for my mom at the café when she'd show up needing work right that minute. If an out-of-luck wanderer showed up asking for food, he'd find a small job for the person to do, too, in exchange for a meal. Kirk's was the place you took the family for a burger and fries and a good time.

My mom wasn't fond of turning her tips and paycheck over to Meta. She had different ideas of what life might hold for her. Plus, she had to hold back some of her tips to buy cigarettes, which Meta would have never allowed. The family she'd grown up with had become too constricting for this naïve seventeen-year-old who yearned for all that life had to hold.

My dad, Joe, was a nice-looking, smooth-talking con man who had served prison time right at the end of World War II. He went to Kirk's Café every day for coffee and pie or a big breakfast of toast, eggs, bacon, and pancakes. My mom served his coffee while he served up endless helpings of compliments.

"The most beautiful girls in the world are redheads," he told her. "There's not a finer waitress in this town, you know!" The charming was endless, and my mom, coming from a strict, domineering mother, soaked up every word that spilled from the mouth of this cunning twenty-eight-year-old charmer.

My mom's family warned her, "Don't marry him. He's been in prison. He's a liar, and you'll regret it if you do." No one was ever able to find out why he'd been in prison but only knew it was at the end of World War II. He had a smooth cover story for everything. He'd been wrongly accused, of course. The promise of freedom from an overbearing household blinded my mom to the less savory side of my dad's personality. When she turned eighteen, she went off and married him, thus taking her first steps down a road of misery and heartache.

They bought a little shack of a house in the low-income Norton-Froehlich area outside of Sioux Falls. Norton sat on one side of a paved road, and Froehlich sat on the other. They were both impoverished areas in those days, but the Norton side, where we lived, was widely considered to be more run down. The area, often referred to as Norton-Froehlich, was comprised of very small homes as well as some made from Federal Army barracks that had been chopped down and hauled to the area for low-income housing. Many homes were unkempt, and here and there an abandoned home with plywood nailed over the doors and windows all created the look of a hopeless shanty town in many sections. Some people worked to make their little home look presentable, yet a lot of this area was dilapidated. The improvements were like the old saying, "putting lipstick on a pig."

Wanda Wulff was my age but grew up on the Froehlich side. In fourth grade, she was invited to a friend's birthday party in the Norton area. When Wanda arrived, she was shocked at the rundown condition of the house. When the friend asked her to get something from the pantry, Wanda came to a complete stop when she saw that it contained only a dirt floor. Even as a nine-year-old, she hesitated to eat the food in the house and left her cake sitting untouched on the plate.

After many years, my parents built a small addition onto our house. At least some of the supplies were stolen from my dad's job at the stockyards as it provided a steady supply of boards and plywood. My dad was a fast talker and cunning, as well. He came across like a good guy who remembered the names of everyone's kids and showed false interest in the lives of his acquaintances—usually as a means of procuring favors from them in return for what usually turned out to be empty or half-promises. Behind closed doors, he abused and degraded his family. He used up the money needed for bills and groceries for his drinking, gambling, and other women, and he left my mom to figure out how to stretch her meager tip money to support three kids—my two older sisters and me.

"You're the ugliest woman I've ever been with! You're not fit to be a mother! You're worthless!" he'd bellow while lashing out physically just to make his point. My mom's fiery spirit took a daily beating until she began to believe my dad's ugly, stabbing words. There were no safe houses for abused women and children in those days. After endless warnings from her family to stay away from him, she was too humiliated to now return to her mother's house. Plus, she was stubborn and determined to prove her worth. So we all stayed for his abuse.

My mom just wanted to be loved, complimented, and taken on a date now and then. Many nights she sat at the kitchen table with a small mirror redoing her hair, freshening her make-up, and dropping hints about the great food at Giovanni's restaurant.

"I'll be back. I'm running to the store," my dad said as he made a quick exit from the house dressed in a good shirt and reeking of cheap after-shave. The crunch from his car tires grew more and more distant as he careened down the street. My mom sat in front of the small mirror and pushed small strands of hair this way and that, changed necklaces, rearranged the containers on the counter, and glanced out the window every time a car passed on the street before eventually changing into pajamas and silently withdrawing to the couch 'til the wee hours of the morning with only a romance novel for company. He got off work at 2:00 on Friday afternoon and sometimes didn't come back until Sunday night.

One week, my mom's Irish temper took a particularly fiery turn.

"We haven't gone out as a family in ages. I know you just got your check and the bills are paid!"

"Clean up and we'll do something tonight," my old man said, to our incredible surprise.

"Where are we going?" I asked my mom.

"Oh, probably Giovanni's or maybe the truck stop. Then we'll maybe go to a drive-in movie," my mom said in a cheery voice as she prepared to pick out a nice outfit, quickly brush and spray her hair, and apply fresh lipstick before my dad changed his mind. We piled into our beat-up, green Plymouth station wagon, and my dad drove toward downtown. He parked in front of a tiny building with cracked stucco siding. It was the Hamburger Inn. An icon for generations, the place was a greasy hamburger joint devoid even of booths. Customers bellied up to the counter on one of the ten stools. The tiny burgers were fifteen cents each and served on a piece of waxed paper set directly on the counter.

"You can order two hamburgers each," my dad told us. My mom's face screwed up into a tight ball. She turned her back to my dad and sat legs crossed and arms folded chain-smoking cigarettes and refusing to eat. "You think you're too good for a burger?" My dad laughed. "Mmmm, aren't these burgers good?" he asked me.

"Yeah! They're good!" I answered enthusiastically, not aware as an eight-year-old that the meal hadn't matched my mom's expectations.

"When we're done eating, I have another treat for us. I guarantee you'll be entertained," he promised.

19

After a quick meal, we drove to the parking lot of Lee and Gordy's Auto and Towing to view the remains of a fatal car wreck. It was a common and macabre event in the 1960s to leave the vehicle of death on display. We eased into a parking space near the spot where the wreck was roped off. Over a dozen people were standing around gawking and whispering.

"You're in for a real treat tonight. Two people were killed in the car over there," he explained. My mom stayed in the car while I eagerly exited, and the opposing forces of the excitement in my dad's voice collided with the grim disgust of realizing what had happened in the horrible car crash.

"They went right under the back end of a flatbed semi!"

The floodlights cast eerie shadows on the tangled mess of twisted metal. The seats, dashboard, and windows were splattered with globs of dried blood. Sprays of broken glass from the shattered windshield littered the insides. Strands of human hair hung from jagged glass. We walked around the vehicle for a good ten minutes, and before we were done I felt ill and frightened. The excitement had evaporated, but I didn't dare show my fear.

Once we got back home, my dad took off again as soon as we were out of the car. My mom's date was over. The mood turned even more somber, and my mom spent the rest of the night at the kitchen table smoking and staring into the distance with a look of heartbroken sadness on her face. The fire was gone from her eyes. My dad didn't come home for two days.

Here is my mom with my dad when she was young and optimistic. After years of living with him, she became an angry and bitter person.

This photo is from the Norton side. It was abandoned structures like this that frightened me at night.

This photo, also from the Norton section, shows a unique decorating style.

Habits

Norton-Froehlich had its share of kind, caring people and determined parents with goals in their lives. Some worked hard in the packing house. Yet, I grew up around so many violent and dysfunctional people that it made a lasting impact on my personality. Fistfighting was our preferred method for solving problems. We established our pecking order this way, and this mind-set became a habit hard to break as I grew older. Many men I knew had hard looks, hard hearts, and some had done hard time. Women with wary eyes and foul mouths took a lot of abuse from these hard men.

As far back as I can remember it seems that my life was one fight after another. There's an old saying among people who train dogs that if a dog bites when it's a pup, it will bite when it's grown. When I was three years old, my mom and I were at my aunt's house, and I was playing with her little dog, Buttons, a dog that was mean and often bit people. I was behind the couch when they heard Buttons begin to yelp and whine. My aunt yelled, "Philip, what did you do to that dog?"

From behind the couch I answered, "I bite him."

"Why did you bite that dog?" my aunt asked.

"He bite me, so I bite him back."

"Where did you bite him?"

"I bite his tail," I answered without remorse. Whenever my mom retold this story, she did so with pride. Fighting back was a valued commodity in my neighborhood. And I lived by this flawed philosophy for years.

By the time I was ten years old, it was second nature to scan the area ahead of me whenever I walked down the streets of Norton. I never let my mind wander but rather walked intently listening for anything out of the ordinary, my head darting from side to side. *No neighborhood bullies on the street today. No vicious dogs off their chains. I can keep walking. For now.* Yet, I always had a plan ready if an unexpected situation arose. *I can run through that yard to escape. If a dog comes charging out of nowhere, I can jump on top of that parked car or climb that tree.* These habits were skills acquired after being schooled in the hard-knock life of Norton-Froehlich.

I had been attacked by vicious dogs, beaten up by bullies, and once even taken to the hospital emergency room for multiple stitches after a group of bullies had beaten me and pulled me over the top of broken glass. There were no sidewalks, only dirt roads that led to grassy or weedy lawns. Occasionally gravel was hauled in, but it was never enough to cover the roads. After a rain, the streets were muddy and pocked with ruts. The dusty driveways were often lined with trash incinerators and junk that provided convenient hiding spots for dogs. Or bullies.

I avoided walking past the abandoned houses because I thought the bogeyman lived in them. Who knows? Maybe he did. Donald Moeller, one of the scary bullies from my neighborhood, often did hang out in the abandoned houses which he used as places to hide his stolen goods. He'd threatened to kill me and other people in the neighborhood. Once he threatened me with a heavy stick because he thought I was shooting my BB gun too close to his house. Donald endured a horrible childhood filled with physical and verbal abuse as well as neglect in the form of a filthy home and lack of food. There was talk in the neighborhood of strange sexual activity in their home. His mother walked around the house naked and had many different men over.

School was no escape for Donald either. There was a cruel science teacher who made his own lye soap and humiliated Donald for coming to school dirty. "Moeller! Come up to this sink and demonstrate to the class how a filthy pig can clean up!" Donald had to scrub his neck, ears, hands, and arms in front of the entire class. All the hurt in his life molded Donald into a violent and angry deviant. He used weapons such as bicycle chains to attack people and was charged with several sexual assaults. Years later, he abducted a nine-year-old girl and raped and sodomized her before slitting her throat. For this crime, he was later executed in the South Dakota State Penitentiary.

I was afraid to stay home alone at night, afraid someone would break in. I became a light sleeper, waking at the sound of every car door or noise on the street, a habit that follows me to this day.

We'd been away fishing for the day. It was a good excuse for my dad to do some boozing while at the same time getting free food for the family. As soon as we walked in the door, it was obvious something was wrong. There were dirty, muddy footprints on the floors and on our beds. Right away, someone noticed the four guns were missing from the gun rack on the wall.

"It was that worthless Donny Moeller from down the street. If the sheriff doesn't go get him, I will!" my dad yelled. It was one of the few times he was right.

We didn't have much of value, but Donny had stolen two of our shotguns, two of our rifles, a couple hunting knives, and a junky space toy of mine. He had also burglarized other homes and businesses prior to that, so when he was finally caught a couple days later selling stolen goods, they found his stash in one of the abandoned homes. The sheriff called to tell my dad that items matching the description of our stolen goods had been recovered, and we got most of the stuff back except for one of our .22 rifles, which was used as court evidence at Donald's trial. It was eventually returned to us, too. I still have that rifle today. Donny was sentenced to the State Training School in Plankinton, SD until he was eighteen.

The charred remains of a burned-down home served as a grim reminder of heartbreak and misery. Its soot-blackened frame stood there for a long time.

25

One day my dad took me to see the burned-out house and told me that a mother had passed out while smoking a cigarette which then started the fire. She was able to escape the blaze but suffered severe burns. Her three young children, however, perished. The smell of the burned house made me sick to my stomach and to this day, my stomach convulses at this reminder of death when I smell a structure fire.

On the Norton side, my own home life was filled with a dismal atmosphere of verbal and physical abuse. My dad was a self-centered drunk who went on two- or three-day binges, spending his money on booze, gambling, and other women. He had a long history of violence and abuse. He had already destroyed his first marriage and in its wake left my two half-sisters and a half-brother. My half-sisters lived with us for a time, and my dad was especially cruel to the girls.

"You fat cows stay out of the refrigerator!" he'd yell at them.

Crack! The back of his hand sent my sister's head snapping in the opposite direction if he thought she'd eaten too much food.

When he left for a weekend of drinking, I never slept soundly. I was afraid he'd come home and beat someone or burn the place down if he passed out smoking. My mom waitressed late into the night, and many times my older sisters would be gone for the evening, too. I had to learn ways to make myself feel safe. When I couldn't fall asleep alone, my only sense of security came from having a loaded rifle in bed with me. This rifle as my bed partner gave me enough peace of mind to drift off to sleep. Some nights I was consumed with devising ways to protect myself.

"If someone did break in, you'd just be giving them the weapon to kill you with," my mom would tell me. But she never told me I couldn't sleep with it.

Mean Dog, Mean Dad

"Your turn. Get on and hold on." When my dad said something, I obeyed.

I reluctantly lay down on the rickety metal runner sled which was attached to the rear bumper of our pickup truck with a thirty-foot length of rope. I braced myself, trying to glue my body to the sled by hooking my feet at the bottom, gripping the frozen metal front with my hands, and wishing I could take off my slippery mittens for a tighter hold. My dad hopped into the truck smiling, revved the engine, shifted into drive, and took off down the country road with me weaving behind on the sled.

"Slow down!" I screamed. We were careening wildly down the snow-packed road and the faster the pickup went, the more the sled shook and vibrated until it was nearly out of control. I could feel the sled yearning to flip me to the side, but I clung with the willpower that can only come from the adrenaline rush felt by someone who'd already experienced the piercing pain of road burns. We skidded over a patch of dry highway, and the metal runners screeched and scraped, jolting the sled sideways. Sparks flew behind me, shooting out like a grinding wheel, but I clung on.

The previous winter we'd done the same thing. I'd walked with a limp for a long time after the sled I'd been riding flipped over and threw me onto the highway like a rag doll. The impact left a huge knot of a bruise on my thigh.

"Good thing you didn't hit your head," was all my dad had said . . . which was true. I never knew of anyone, including us, whoever wore a helmet for any activity. I've often wondered how some children, myself included, ever made it through childhood without serious injury. It's events like this that make people believe in guardian angels.

****

Barney wasn't the most ferocious dog in the neighborhood, but he definitely had a nasty side. He was a large German shepherd who lived one block north of our place. What did make Barney stand out was that he was all white with a pinkish nose. I often hung around with the kid who owned Barney, and whenever I went to his place, I made sure the dog was on his chain before going up to the door.

As usual, I was outside one afternoon getting ready for my first sled ride of the day on a hillside not far from our house. At my side was the same sled that my dad used to pull us behind the pickup truck. I flopped down on my stomach and was just poised to go down the hill, when to my left I caught sight of Barney loping along toward me. All of a sudden he had appeared out of nowhere. *Oh no! What's he doing off the chain?* The only place I could go to get away was downhill, so I pushed off and began picking up a little speed as I started inching down the hill. I cranked my head back, hoping to see that Barney had moved along or disappeared, but there he was racing toward me. The movement of my sled must have caught Barney's attention, and he went from a lope to a full Olympic sprint, headed right for me. He was on me in a flash, snapping and snarling at my face as he raced alongside my sled. I held up my arm to shield my face and held tight to the sled with the other hand. I kept trying to twist my head away from him, but one of his bites latched onto my ear. After a few more bites, my sled picked up enough speed and Barney backed off.

When the sled came to a stop, I pulled off my mittens and reached up to find that he'd ripped part of my ear lobe away from my head. Warm blood ran through my fingers, down my neck, and spattered onto the snow beneath me. I glanced back, and Barney was trotting off in another direction. Tears welled in my eyes, but I fought them back and grabbed handfuls of snow to rub on my torn ear. When the snow finally melted into a dark crimson color, I flicked the mess onto the ground and started over until the bleeding stopped.

Back home I examined the damaged ear in the mirror and decided that I did not need stitches. I plastered the edges together with bandages instead. My mom noticed the injury and questioned me about it, assuming I'd gotten in another fight. I told her I'd hit some bushes riding on my sled. I didn't want my dad to find out what had happened because he might get a whim to use it as an excuse to shoot the dog if he ever saw Barney loose near our house. I didn't think it was all Barney's fault since his owners should have kept a better eye on him instead of letting him run loose.

****

My dad was an expert at saving a buck any way he could, especially on the grocery bill. When late summer rolled around, he'd take us out to a remote farm field right after dark set in to steal sweet corn. On this particular day, he drove just far enough outside the city limits until he found an access road into a field where he could hide the car. It wasn't a corn field though, so we had to walk down a gravel road, each of us prepared with a paper sack. My dad stood watch at the edge of the field while my sister and I pulled ears of corn off the stalks as fast as we could, wanting to fill our sacks and get out of there.

My sack wasn't yet half full when my dad yelled, "Car!" He came rushing into the field to herd us back a few rows where we'd be hidden from the road. The car whizzed by, and we continued picking. I felt certain it was the farmer's car and that they'd noticed us there. I pictured the farmer driving to his farmhouse, grabbing a gun, and coming back after us.

"Better hurry up. Farmers shoot and kill people all the time for stealing corn," my dad claimed. As a nine-year-old, I didn't realize how preposterous that was. My stomach clenched and churned. I was certain that every sound I heard was a farmer sneaking up on us with a gun.

"You okay?" my sister asked.

I nodded even while I choked back the fear that was rising from my stomach. I had a bad feeling something was about to happen, yet I didn't stop picking. I forced myself to focus on keeping a steady hand to perform under pressure. With our bags finally overflowing, we must have been a sight, all of us in a line speed walking while each carrying a paper grocery bag along a dark dirt road. I breathed a sigh of relief when we reached the car and stashed the corn out of sight in the trunk. Everything was okay now. Little did I know the night was not yet over.

We were almost home when my dad pulled into the unlocked cemetery near our neighborhood and drove down the inky dark road with the only light coming from the headlamps' reflection as they bounced off the gravestones that flashed in and out of sight with an eerie silence. The stories he'd told us about crazy people who went into cemeteries and dug up bodies flashed through my head.

"I heard people have seen ghouls and ghosts around here at night. I bet they're all over on a night like this," he hissed.

No one spoke. My dad eased the car to the top of a hill and came to stop in the dead center of the cemetery. We knew what was coming next. It was one of my dad's favorite pastimes when he needed a drink and was feeling extra mean.

"Out of the vehicle," he ordered. None of us ever considered saying no, and my sister silently slid out next to the vehicle. Tonight, for some reason, I stayed put, refusing to budge. Without saying a word, my dad got out of the car, came around to my side, took hold of my upper arm and yanked me out with me fumbling to find my footing.

He drove away and all we could do was watch the tail lights eventually fade to darkness.

"Come back!" I screamed, running after him into near blackness, trying to stay on the road and not run off onto the grass and into a headstone.

"Stay behind me! Run fast and we'll get to the car," my sister said, trying to comfort me. But she was older and faster and seemed to be a million miles ahead while I was left behind with ghosts and skeletons who closed in from behind ready to grab me and pull me to their underground home, where I'd never be found again. I made myself concentrate on running hard and not stumbling. If I fell, it would just take longer to get out.

When we finally reached the car just outside the cemetery, my dad was behind the wheel laughing hysterically. The car smelled of whiskey. My heart was pounding. But I'd done it. I hadn't overcome my fears, but they hadn't overcome me, either. Fear and I would meet again many times until I eventually came to realize that some things could only hurt me if I let them.

I often wondered what made my dad so mean. Years later I asked my uncle Mel, my dad's brother, what made my dad be the way he was.

"Your dad was always nuts. Even as a kid he was mean to other kids and animals. He'd hide around the shed when I had a friend over, and would step out and bust the kid in the nose for no reason and knock the kid on his rear. One time I had a friend over and we were standing next to the barn when all of a sudden we were getting peed on. We looked up, and it was your dad standing in the loft, laughing and peeing on us. I asked your grandma if she dropped him on his head when he was a baby. He's so mean and crazy. Your grandma just shook her head and said nothing." I despised my dad yet didn't realize how often I followed his same footsteps.

Boom, Boom, Boom!

I tossed two plastic green army men on top of the growing pile of odds and ends in the paper grocery bag I'd put next to the back steps. I'd been adding to the collection all week. I took a few steps, just far enough to see down the street, and craned my head sideways, hoping the car I was waiting for would finally come into view. Still nothing. My cousin Doug from Minnesota was coming to stay with us for a few days, then we'd drive him back home on our way to the annual Fourth of July reunion.

By the time Doug arrived, I was so excited I practically dragged him from the car, slapped a pack of matches in his hand, and led him to the arsenal I'd accumulated in the paper bag.

Kaboom! The first casualty was a rusty soup can that soared into the air, catapulted with a loud pop by the small twist of firecrackers that had exploded beneath it. We spent the afternoon devising various ways to blow up the pile of odds and ends we'd now placed onto the dirt patch that was our launching pad. Doug twisted two or three firecracker wicks together trying to get them to explode simultaneously, which would result in a big explosion. The sun beat down on our bare backs through the light smoke that hovered above us, and the distinctly acrid smell of fireworks filled the yard.

Tired of roasting in the midday sun, we moved our operation to the shade of a silver maple and built a fort using only dirt and gravel. We placed all the toy soldiers around the fort, then lit firecrackers, which we called hand grenades, and threw them at the enemy. If a blast toppled a soldier, we would cheer and whoop. After much experimentation, we developed a bazooka, which was a lead water pipe with a bottle rocket as the explosive round. We'd sight down the pipe, aiming like a rifle. One of us would be the assistant gunner who would place and light the bottle rocket.

"Ahh! It got me again!" Doug shouted, batting at the sparks from the back blast that had burned the side of this face.

Without hesitation, I lit another bottle rocket. We were having too much fun to worry about small injuries. The firecrackers were a more serious concern, however. They were more powerful at that time with my favorite brands— Black Cat, Zebra, and Shotgun—all packing potentially harmful doses of gunpowder. There was only one time that I held a firecracker too long, and it exploded in my hand. The blast split one of my fingertips open, left a huge blood blister on another finger, and caused a numb tingling sensation through my palm. I ran, blowing on my fingertips, into the house.

"Don't come crying to me if you hold one of those firecrackers!" my mom scolded but rubbed my fingers with butter and wrapped them in gauze, all the while yelling at me for dripping blood in the house.

One Fourth of July, Doug burned his eye, and I burned my hand on a sparkler. Doug had to wear a white gauze eye patch, and I had my hand heavily wrapped in white bandages. Yet these injuries didn't deter two explosives experts like us. In the late afternoon, we sat in the blazing hot July sun eating cold watermelon and sporting assorted injuries, filthy with grime, and smelling like gunpowder. Even though we were now old enough to know it wasn't true, we'd been raised to be careful not to eat any watermelon seeds lest we end up with "watermelon belly." Whenever a female relative showed up with a swelling midsection, we were told it was due to swallowing watermelon seeds. I had some relatives who ended up with "watermelon belly" when they should have been more careful with seeds.

****

Carroll Lee was a fun-loving stock car racing fan who was a big kid at heart. He was my second cousin and the father of seven young children. He supported his lively family by driving a bulldozer at the city dump. He frequently unearthed perfectly good items there such as chairs or cabinets that someone had thrown away. Carroll Lee would hop off the bulldozer and retrieve the item, which he'd later bring home. One fortunate day just before the Fourth of July, he discovered two huge crates filled with fireworks that the city had discarded for unknown reasons. He brought the fireworks to our place in Norton-Froehlich since our house was outside the city limits. He figured out how to ignite the aerial displays using a large steel tube, long electrical wire, and an electric battery. The adults discussed the possible instability of these projectiles and finally decided everyone should hide behind the cars about thirty yards away while Carroll Lee detonated the fireworks.

BOOM! BOOM! BOOM! The first display soared into the air, showering a beautiful spray of colored lights overhead. We oohed and aahed, until nothing but wisps of steely smoke were left in the air clouding our thoughts with the idea that perhaps the gunpowder was reliable after all. Carroll Lee waited until everyone was safely tucked behind their respective cars before setting off the next round. There was a loud hiss and then a mighty explosion which sent sparks and shrapnel barreling into the vehicles that were thankfully shielding us. Next to me, my dad was swearing a blue streak. The blast had split the side window on his old pickup truck. I rubbed my ears to stop the ringing but could still hear my aunt yelling at Carroll Lee to stop before someone got killed. So, that was the end of our free fireworks display courtesy of the city and Carroll Lee's sharp eyes.

"You'll Shoot Your Eye Out!"

POP! POP! POP! That was a small caliber weapon.

BANG! That was a shotgun.

CRACK! The sound of a high-powered rifle really got my attention because a 30-06 projectile had the power to go through a house provided it only hit drywall or paneling and not a beam. It can kill someone three miles away. In the Norton section, the sound of gunfire occurred periodically, and with my previous hunting experience, I became adept at identifying the type of weapon fired. Our neighborhood sat outside of the city limits and people would fire off weapons for a variety of generally irresponsible reasons. At times, people who were drunk just blasted off weapons. Stray dogs were sometimes shot at by an angry homeowner tired of dealing with a snarling hound digging through the garbage or threatening the children. One of our dogs had been shot and killed by a shotgun blast, and we never did find out who had done it. Since we lived close to fields, some people would target practice right out of their back door. Some neighbors were responsible gun owners, but others were foolish and irresponsible with their weapons. I fell into the latter category and did some incredibly stupid things involving firearms.

School was out for the summer, and now eighth grade was a fading memory. I went over to my friend Jim's house, knocked on the door, opened it up, and let myself in.

"Hey, Jim! I'm here," I yelled.

"I'm in the back room on the phone. Come on in," he responded.

When I got to the rear of his house, I saw Jim standing with the phone to his ear bantering back and forth with his brother. I sat down on his bed and waited for him to hang up, but, unfortunately, sitting quietly isn't one of my strengths. They say that curiosity kills the cat, and I was about to find that out the hard way. I noticed a rifle I hadn't seen before leaning against the wall. I picked it up to look it over. It was one of the new style BB guns that had a pump hand grip instead of a single cock lever. If the handle was pumped over and over, increased air pressure built up in the cylinder, making this weapon as deadly as a .22 rifle. While Jim talked on the phone with his back to me, I decided to pull a prank on him. I pumped the rifle up several times building air pressure. *I better make sure it's not loaded* ran through my mind. I pulled the bolt back and checked to see if a BB was in the chamber. Nope, no BB in there. So, I figured my prank was harmless. I was not familiar with this new style weapon and didn't know it had a new automatic BB feed that loaded the gun when the bolt was pulled back. By pulling the bolt back, I had armed this rifle without knowing it even though the feed had been empty when I'd checked.

At first I was going to blow Jim's hair up in the back of his head, but at the last second decided blowing air into his butt would be much more humorous. Jim was laughing away with his back turned to me when I placed the barrel right up to his butt and squeezed the trigger. POP! The gun spit out a loud sound.

Jim's body went rigid; he let out a loud shriek then dropped the phone and collapsed to the floor where he lay moaning. I thought he was faking, but then stood frozen with shock as a pool of blood began spreading across the back of Jim's blue jeans while he squirmed on the floor in agony. Moments later he let loose with a slew of swear words, calling me one name after another. He managed to stand on bent, wobbly legs clutching his rear end with his left hand. I moved over toward him and was suddenly met with a tremendous punch to the left side of my face. Jim had hauled off and hit me, and I knew I deserved it. He called his mom to come pick him up and bring him to the hospital, so I left, figuring there was no reason for me to stick around and get yelled at.

Jim had to have surgery to remove the BB followed by a round of antibiotics to ward off infections. I had to talk with a deputy sheriff who was investigating the shooting. He chewed me out for my stupidity, and again I knew I deserved it. He told me to never horse around with a firearm. Just like in one of my favorite Christmas movies, people used to tell us, "Be careful or you'll shoot your eye out!" I knew one kid who lost a front tooth and another who really did get his eye shot out and had a glass eye from BB gun fights. I was just thankful I hadn't decided to puff up Jim's hair with a head shot.

****

Evidently, I didn't learn my lesson the first time around. My buddy Ron came over to my house with his .22 rifle to show me the new scope he'd had mounted on it. When he handed me the rifle, I pointed it out our front window and looked through the scope at the crosshairs.

"Nice scope," I said and then pulled the trigger without a second thought. I was stunned when a loud *BANG* echoed through the room, and we were suddenly standing frozen before a window streaked with giant cracks that spread from a golf-ball–sized hole.

"What the hell are you doing handing me a loaded rifle in the house?" I yelled.

"What are doing firing that gun without checking to see if it was loaded?" he bellowed back just as loudly.

When my mom came home, she screamed louder than both of us combined when she saw the shattered window standing as a testament to our poor decision-making skills. We didn't have a lot of extra money, and now because of another stupid firearm mishap my mom had to replace a window.

****

Third time's a charm, right? I was pheasant hunting with my friend Tim. Neither of us had much money, so this was a real treat to spend the night in a drive-up motel in the small town of Platte, South Dakota, and hunt pheasants for two days. It was picture-perfect pheasant country with its fields of golden grass on a gently rolling landscape.

"You go down to the far end of the field as a blocker so the birds don't run out the other end, and I'll walk through the field."

Tim loaded his shotgun and headed to the far end of the field. When he was in place, I began slowly walking through the waist-high grass. I hadn't gone twenty yards when a spray of pheasants flushed up into the air.

POW! POW! The shotgun's stock slammed into my shoulder from the recoil. One pheasant went down. I could also hear an occasional *POP* as Tim shot at pheasants on his end of the field. I continued walking, and when I got within twenty-five yards of where Tim was positioned, several pheasants swarmed up from the side of the field on our flank. A bird flushed up to my right. I aimed, and just as I pulled the trigger, I saw Tim standing there. Without letting me know, he had moved from his position in front of me to my right. Too late. The shotgun fell from his hands, and he dropped to his knees, stunned by the buckshot that had blasted him in the face, chest, stomach, and arms. Everything happened instantaneously. I raced over to Tim and saw blood dripping through his hands as he held his face, swearing.

"You son-of-a-bitch! You shot me!" he yelled.

"Buddy, I didn't see you! What are you doing over here? You're supposed to be in your blocking position! Let's get you to a doctor," I shouted.

We rushed back to the car and barreled down gravel roads to a rural medical clinic, where they controlled the bleeding and removed as much of the shot as they could. My biggest concern was his face, and Tim's biggest concern was some painful buckshot lodged between the tendons in the back of his hand.

They got almost everything out except for a few that were too deep to reach, and Tim carries them in his body to this day. For a second time, I had to talk to a sheriff about shooting someone. It was foolish for Tim to leave his position, and stupid of me to pull the trigger before knowing exactly where the projectiles would end up. To this day, Tim and I debate about who was mostly at fault for this shooting. Even after these events, I maintain that firearms are not the problem. It's people who make foolish decisions or allow kids access to weapons that cause firearm mishaps.

Boozin' Abuser

"You stupid little bitch!" I heard my dad bellow from the other room as I stepped into our house. I peeked around the corner to find that he was yelling at my sister.

"You're worthless and can't do a damn thing right, can you?" *SLAP*. She got his right hand across the back of her head. No matter what she said or did, I knew it wouldn't be right since he needed to find some way to blame her in order to justify his abuse. The two of them were working on adding a small addition to the kitchen. Over the years, many people in Norton-Froehlich had begun improving or adding on to their homes, and decades later many of the original structures were torn down and replaced completely. My sisters were older and along with my mom were responsible for almost all the work around the house. The girls were expected to be home right after school while I was at least allowed to participate in sports. My dad was especially cruel to females, and my blood would boil when he used his strength and position to dominate our family in despicable ways. I imagined being tough enough to hit him like he did to us. Eventually, an urge sprung forth from this. *If only I were strong enough to protect us.*

I helped my dad at times, too, but never had the patience for holding nails or making careful measurements and became frequently distracted. I was helping him with a fence and didn't hold the post straight enough when it was getting placed into the ground. *WHACK*. He slammed the hammer handle across the middle of my back. When I turned, he kicked my tailbone so hard I sunk to the ground.

"Ha ha ha. You're movin' like an old man!" he laughed at me when I struggled to walk.

43

I couldn't move my legs without excruciating pain, but he laughed at the way I walked for the rest of the day. It was getting close to the end of the week, and his anger surfaced more quickly when it was almost time to hit the bars for one of his two-day drunks. He often returned with a sob story to gain our sympathy or became overly apologetic if he'd promised to take me hunting but disappeared for the weekend instead. Many times I went to bed on a Friday night so excited that I could hardly sleep anticipating the next day's pheasant or deer hunt. I'd bound out of bed Saturday morning to find the house quiet and my dad still gone. I learned not to trust people. As the week rolled on he became mean and violent again when he started needing his booze.

With my dad, it wasn't always physical abuse that hurt, but the emotional rollercoaster we were on with the way he ran his life was upsetting. If he had extra money, we might have plenty of food that week. If he'd lost everything gambling, there'd be next to nothing. He worked at the stockyards and regularly scammed some way for us to have a pig, horse, or sheep. He always had a way to sell them off for profit down the road. One of my escapes was to hide out in the lean-to shed in the backyard with whatever animal we had at the time. Yet, I soon learned that whenever I became attached to an animal, he'd end up selling it.

One day our horse gave birth to a beautiful, brown foal. He told me I could have that horse for my own. I named her Flicka, and we put up a fence around the lean-to where we normally kept pigs. My dad made some kind of deal with a guy from work who was from West River, South Dakota, to break Flicka so I could ride her. This man, a former competition rodeo rider, showed up at our house a few times wearing a big silver buckle on his belt and a plaid cowboy shirt. He green-broke Flicka so I figured she was ready to ride and took off on her bareback one day. She bucked me off and I spent the next few weeks on crutches. I knew it wasn't her fault, though, so I continued petting, brushing, and feeding her sugar cubes until the day I returned home from school about a year later to find my dad had sold her. Eventually, I learned to ignore the animals that showed up in the shed and to be wary of becoming attached to anything too easily.

My dad couldn't go long without finding something that would upset the household. My parents were working on another remodeling project when he flipped out at my mom, grabbed her by the throat, and put the power drill right to her forehead. The drill whined with the sharp bit spinning a mere inch from her face.

"If you don't keep your mouth shut, I'll run this drill though your brain!" his voice boomed through the house. I stood petrified, never sure when he'd snap and actually follow through. At the time, I wished my mom would just be quiet and not provoke his anger. I hadn't developed the maturity yet to fully understand the situation.

My mom sometimes argued back, though. On this particular day, my dad had put on his best shirt and was headed for the door when my mom, who was sitting at the table drinking a bottle of pop, jumped to her feet.

"Go to the bar and see your whores!" she screamed and then threw the pop bottle at him. It shattered against the door jamb right next to his head.

"Bad shot, bitch. Have fun cleaning it up," he laughed and headed to his pickup truck.

He didn't return until Sunday, and my mom sat at the table, staring into space for much of the weekend. When I tried to talk to her, she'd give a small one-word answer and turn away. This is how she dealt with the abuse. My best means of escaping this world of fear and uncertainty was to take our hunting dog down by the river along with my BB gun and just stay away from it all. I frequently felt anxious and had conflicting feelings about evading his wrath while my mom and sisters took the worst of his anger.

My dad sometimes slapped but often used his fists. There were cruel things going on behind closed doors in our house. During one of his violent outbursts, he knocked the front teeth out of one of my sisters. He ordered us to say that she fell against a cement step if any relatives or the police asked about it.

I always worried about whose turn it would be next to suffer at his hands. When I was seven, I began a strange ritual to shift the focus away from the frustration of these troubling thoughts and also to release the stress that had built up inside of me. I would lie with my bare back against the metal grid of our fuel oil heater until I had my own grid of red burn marks across my back. The pain temporarily soothed the chaos writhing within, and in my mind I called it "good pain."

During this time in my life, I was plagued with severe stomachaches that had troubled me since I was a preschooler and kept me awake at night. I made two trips to the hospital where I drank a chalky liquid so the doctors could test my stomach. They never found a physical reason for the stomachaches that continued to haunt me for years. Often when I was in school, the pain would disappear until close to the end of the school day, when the throbbing ache would creep back and prevent me from concentrating on anything the teacher said. At the time, I didn't make the connection. I relieved my anxiety with pain until I was older and found other ways to stop the frustrations.

Brains and a Brainless Stunt

A familiar stink made me wrinkle my nose. The crackle of grease sizzled in the huge iron skillet across the room on the stove. I lifted the lid and confirmed my suspicions. We were having fried liver for dinner. *Yuck!* A minute ago I'd walked into the house starving, but now my appetite was gone. I began plotting ways to get myself out of eating dinner tonight.

The butcher shop sold liver, cow brains, and cow tongue dirt cheap. I hated all three. My mom usually fried the liver in lard topped with chopped up onions. She grew up eating liver and onions and loved it. Most of the time the brains were served mixed with scrambled eggs. Of the three, we had liver the most often. I smothered it in ketchup and ate tiny bites.

Once when a buddy invited me to his place to eat we went inside right when it was time for supper. There on the table sat fried liver. I was afraid to refuse to eat it. I didn't know how his parents would react. They had no ketchup, so I kept taking small bites but then briefly covered my mouth with my hand or turned my head for a moment and put the liver back in my curled palm. On my way home, I fed the pocketed food to a hunting dog who was roaming the street.

When you're poor like many of the folks I lived around, you find other creative ways to save money. My mom took me to a barbershop for haircuts, but several of my friends regularly sported unbelievably crooked bangs. I tried to hold back the laughter once when a friend who typically had a longer haircut showed up with a bowl cut. His mom had put a bowl over his head to use as a guideline and snipped away, leaving him looking like he had a perfect mushroom cap of hair. When he saw me laughing, he started in, too, and we discussed trying to make his hair look better but decided we might actually make it worse.

Some kids ran barefoot in the summer, saving their shoes for the cold weather. I had some aunts and uncles who bought us clothes, but of course, this had to have a down-side, too. Once at the bus stop I got kicked in the rear for wearing a brand new pair of jeans.

"Look at the little pretty boy! Now look at me kick the pretty boy's butt!" the kid taunted me. A few kids snickered, and then it was over. He moved on to someone else.

I was a little hesitant the time I wore a new sweater and nice pants I'd gotten for Christmas. My fear of getting beaten up for dressing like a sissy was never realized, but I got harassed about the clothes for a couple days. It blew over when a kid came to school wearing glasses for the first time. Then it was poor Frog Eye's turn to take some abuse for a while. I began not liking people because of so many experiences with angry, miserable troublemakers who had no capacity for appreciating someone else's happiness.

Holidays can be a notoriously lousy time for dysfunctional families and kids who live in poverty. Instead of anticipating a day of joyful fun, it means more time at home, more time to get abused, and more drunken outbursts to witness. I preferred being at school. School was predictable; home was not. A lot of kids got excited by Christmas, but others became depressed or took their frustration out on others who did get presents. Today when I work with students I'm careful not to ask them what they got for Christmas. I usually say, "What did you like about your school break?" or "Tell me about your school break."

I did love summer vacation, though. I was normally unsupervised and most days I roamed the fields along the Big Sioux River not far from our house with my BB gun. I rode my bike around the neighborhood a lot, too, and a group of us would practice stunts on our bikes. I liked challenging myself, and I liked performing. One day the brilliant thought occurred to me to try a stunt with a fat hog my dad had penned up in our back yard. My dad wasn't around, or I would have been in trouble for messing around with the hog he was getting ready to sell after having fattened it up with feed he'd stolen from his job at the stockyards.

"I can ride that hog all around the pen like a rodeo rider," I bragged to my buddies. I'd never actually tried it, but I was a good athlete, and it looked easy enough to my young eyes.

I climbed over the fence and approached the grunting pig from behind. With a quick hop, I was astride its back and on my way to rodeo fame. My time in the spotlight lasted all of three seconds and five yards. That porker bucked and sprinted out from under me in a flash, tossing me unceremoniously onto my back. I found myself looking up at the clear, blue sky and could hear the howls of laughter from my buddies. I slowly rose to my feet, disgusted by the thick, stinking hog poo which now covered me from head to foot. Fresh hog droppings were caked in my hair and slimy mud-crap slipped down my pants. I thought I'd be entertaining riding that pig, but my friends got the last laugh. I didn't live that one down for years.

You Don't Tell

The warm water felt good splashing onto my neck and shoulders. The rising steam in the shower room soothed my muscles after a day of swimming with my friend Ronnie at Drake Springs swimming pool. The water had been extra cold so we were in the showers getting warmed up. I closed my eyes and let the hot water run over the top of my head. Suddenly, I felt a sharp tap on my shoulder. I turned around, wiped the water from my eyes, and when I opened them, I saw four kids about my age standing in a semicircle around me. The kid closest to me had a sneer on his face and stood with his hands on his hips looking as if he were about to pounce. He had a round scar under his eye and was visibly angry. *This doesn't look good,* I thought.

"Hey, how come you splashed me in the pool?" the angry kid accused.

"I didn't splash anyone," I responded.

"Shut your mouth, smart ass, and keep it shut," he challenged.

I knew they were looking for trouble, and before I could think of a way out of the situation one of his friends shoved me hard from the side. When I turned to see who'd done it, a bright light like a flash from a camera exploded in front of me. My head pulsed, and I realized the light was the impact from him punching me between the eyes. I staggered back a couple of steps and started swinging at the kid who'd just sucker-punched me. No use. Fists that seemed to come from everywhere were landing on my head, face, and neck from all sides. They knocked me to the ground, and I curled into a ball trying to protect myself from a flurry of kicks. I peered between my arms, but all I saw was Ronnie running out the door. After they had their fun, the battering subsided, and I could breathe again.

"All right. He better not splash *me* again," the first kid said as they all ran outside.

51

I staggered to my feet and went over to the shiny rectangle of reflective metal hanging on the wall that served as a mirror. My face looked distorted on the wavy surface, my lips were bleeding, and my ribs throbbed. I wondered if Ronnie had gone to get help as I started to clean myself up. I rinsed my mouth, spitting out blood for several minutes, then headed back to the pool to find Ronnie since no one had shown up to help. I searched until I found Ronnie lying on the cement sun deck as if nothing had happened.

"Man, how come you didn't help me?" I implored.

"I wasn't going to stay around for that. There were too many of them!" he said matter-of-factly.

"I thought you went to get help!"

"I didn't want to run and tattle!"

I didn't say anything. If he had stayed, he would have gotten a beating too. If he'd gone to get help from an adult, both of us would have probably gotten in more trouble for fighting.

****

I was at the age when I started to question whether adults could be trusted to make good decisions, or trusted at all, for that matter. Many times when I went pheasant hunting with my dad, he'd tear down a "No Hunting" sign posted on a fence and toss it into the weeds.

"Now there's not a *No Hunting* sign. Let's go!" he'd say without any apparent concern for getting caught. We never were caught either.

Where I grew up, many disagreements were solved with accusations and threats rather than reason.

"Keep your *&#$@!% dog off our yard or we'll shoot the damn thing!" I heard more than once. Dogs did get shot in our area so I knew it was a real possibility.

As a kid, you repeat what you see modeled. I was alone and unsupervised most of the time and preferred being outside on the streets where something might be happening rather than cooped up at home by myself. One day when I was eleven I ran into Irv Moeller, who lived a few houses away.

"Come with me. I know how we can have some fun," he said.

Irv was older than me and was a tough kid who'd been in trouble with the law before. I followed him down the block, and he led me to a vacant house that was for sale. The back door was wide open, so we went inside without hesitation. Irv walked over to a wall in the kitchen and yelled "Wham!" while landing a fierce sidekick that knocked a big hole in the drywall. Then he kicked two more holes in the wall. It looked fun, so I joined in. We yelled and kicked, littering the floor with chunks of wall and dust, then moved into the kitchen and busted a light fixture. We had no respect for this property that wasn't ours and went to town kicking our way through the house and admiring the damage we'd created. A loud noise from another room stopped us in our tracks. The front door had swung wide open and in walked a middle-aged lady and a man in his twenties. My heart jumped into my throat. Irv and I didn't even look at each other. We split out the back door in a flash, both going in separate directions.

I was lucky, and the older lady chased after me. The young man ran down the street after Irv. I sprinted down another street and cut between two houses into a wooded area not far from where I lived. My feet barely grazed the ground, and I ran past trees and thickets before eventually collapsing in some heavy bushes. I was panting loudly and trying to breathe quietly while remaining hidden until I was convinced it was safe. I didn't see anyone ahead of me so I carefully picked my way back and returned to my house in a roundabout way. I could barely swallow so when I got home, I gulped water and took some deep breaths. I finally felt safe in the security of my house. The feeling was short lived.

I peered out our side window where I could see Irv's house just down the block. To my dismay, two county sheriff's cars were parked in front. Irv had been caught. I sat down on a chair and clutched my stomach, sick with worry knowing at any minute the cops would be at our house to get me. The wait was agonizing. Why had I busted up that house? Each minute seemed like an hour, yet the knock on the door never came. The next time I looked outside, the street was clear. The sheriff's cars were gone and so was Irv.

He'd been hauled away to juvenile detention, and then a short time later was sentenced to forestry camp in the Black Hills of South Dakota. This camp was a boot camp program where offenders had to work clearing dead trees and salvaging wood. Irv was at forestry camp for over a year. When he came back, he told me what he'd said to the cops instead of ratting me out:

"I just told the sheriff that you were some kid I didn't know who was busting up the house, so I went in and did it, too. No way was I going to be a rat."

I knew I owed Irv big. During his stay at forestry camp, Irv got involved in weight lifting and martial arts. He came back an even tougher kid than before. People did not mess with him, and bullies didn't pick on other people when he was around, either. Recently, he said forestry camp was actually good for him. He kept his nose pretty clean after that and to this day holds a steady job.

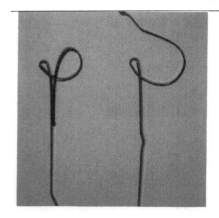

Tools of the trade. These snappers are what bullies used to inflict pain. The one on the left is loaded and ready to snap. The one on the right shows the unleashed position.

Irv Moeller, who came to my defense a few times, was one of the tough guys in the neighborhood. His brother, Donald, one of the neighborhood bullies, was later executed in the state penitentiary for rape and murder.

Messiah Lutheran Church sat between the Norton and Froehlich sections. This church was firebombed one night.

This is the rifle and the knife stolen from our house by Donald Moeller.

Chipper

When I was ten years old, my mom asked me what I wanted for Christmas. Each time she asked I gave the same reply.

"All I want is a monkey."

"They cost too much. Pick something else you want," she kept telling me.

But I stuck with the monkey as my only choice. They sold these tiny squirrel monkeys in pet stores back when I was a kid, but I'm sure they weren't cheap. My mom probably pinched pennies for weeks until she came up with enough cash to buy me the monkey I'd begged for. On Christmas Eve while I was at my aunt's house, my mom sent my dad to the pet store to get the little guy. As usual, my dad had a way of messing up a simple thing. After he had picked up the monkey at the pet store, he stopped by his job site to show off the monkey to some co-workers, most likely taking the credit for buying this fabulous gift. Evidently, he hadn't made sure the cage was tightly latched. While my dad was inside gathering his co-workers, Chipper escaped from the cage and unbeknownst to my dad, was loose in the car. My dad returned with a throng of people all anxious to get a look at the exotic pet. When my dad opened the car door, the monkey shot out like a flash. By sheer luck, my dad grabbed the monkey just before he made his final escape into a cold, snowy parking lot where he would have surely died before the night was over. Chipper was returned to the cage and carted home immediately.

"I got a monkey!" I screamed to my sisters when I saw his wide smile and mouth full of teeth. This was a Christmas morning I relished as this adorable monkey chattered excitedly.

We all quickly became attached to him. When I let Chipper out of his cage just to play with him, I could never catch him to put him back. I had to lure him into his cage with fruit or seeds. He didn't like being picked up. He had to

57

decide when he wanted to go and sit on someone's lap. He'd curl up by me on the couch, and I'd feed him treats. Then he'd run around the house, grab the curtains, scamper up them in a second, and run across the curtain rods where he'd leap to a shelf or table and continue flying around the house before suddenly disappearing from sight.

I'm not sure what unfolded between my dad and that little monkey on Christmas Eve, the night he almost escaped to the cold parking lot of the work site. It was probably due to the fact that my dad had to grab him and squeeze him to keep him from escaping, or maybe he could sense that my dad was just a bad person. Whatever the reason, Chipper had hated my dad from day one and would hiss and rattle his cage whenever my dad entered the room. Once my dad was fighting with my mom, and Chipper was screeching away at my dad, as usual.

"I'll let that monkey out on you!" my mom threatened. And a minute later she did.

Chipper was extremely quick, and he raced all over the house, sprinted under the table, and leaped about until finally landing on my dad's back, sinking his teeth into the old man's shoulder. Then it was my dad who let out a screech and began hopping up and down trying to shake his tiny attacker loose. No use. Chipper danced around like a drop of water on a hot pan. He jumped off on his own accord after a few good bites. Then my dad chased Chipper to no avail as that monkey scampered here and there before disappearing like a ghost. My dad eventually gave up and headed to the bar.

I knew my mom had worked hard to get me such a memorable gift, and I'm sure it had to do with the fact that her childhood was shrouded in extreme poverty during the Great Depression. As a child, my mom and her siblings got only one gift at Christmas and that was the one handed out by the Salvation Army. She worked hard to make our Christmases special by seeing that we got at least one thing we really wanted and by baking holiday pies, bars, and cookies though all the while complaining that Christmas was too much work.

Chipper was a bright spot, yet it seemed like every bright event had to have an equal and opposite dark side. If we had a family reunion, there was fighting. If we built an addition onto our house, someone got beaten. If I got a new coat, some jealous kid threw me to the ground trying to rip it. Chipper was no exception. In order to save on the heating bills, my mom turned the heat down during the day in the winter. Chipper developed a monkey cold, coughing and wheezing and bringing a pang of worry to my stomach when he tilted his head while peering up at me with big, sad eyes. A vet would have cost too much money. I'd listen to him breathe when he'd take a pause from running around the house to lay his head on my shoulder and convinced myself he seemed to be getting better. I went to his cage every morning to bring him breakfast, and one morning I approached his cage and knew immediately that he was dead.

I learned more about caring for animals with every passing year. For starters, exotic pets often require extraordinary care. After that, I stuck to dogs and became very attentive to their needs. And I never asked for another monkey or any other unusual pets no matter how much I thought I wanted one.

Where There's Smoke

The relentless wind was forcing its way through every crack in our aging house, its low howl a reminder of the fierce blizzard still battering the streets outside. A half-moon of crusty snow had formed at the base of the front window, and when I peered outside, I couldn't even see to the edge of the yard. All I saw was swirling white. The blizzard had been raging without a break for two days. Some people had chains to wrap around their car tires so they could maneuver the streets if absolutely necessary. We didn't. Snow drifts were so high in spots that we weren't able to drive half a block without becoming stuck in a snow bank.

I sat back down to watch TV and noticed my mom roaming from room to room rummaging through each of the six ashtrays spread throughout the house and muttering. Next, she dumped all the butts onto the kitchen table. I got up from the couch, curious.

"What are you doing?" I asked.

"I ran out of cigarettes because of this damn storm."

She proceeded to take out every cigarette butt, checking each one over meticulously to see if there were still a couple of puffs left. I shook my head in disbelief when she began lighting each butt and inhaling deeply until every speck of tobacco had disappeared in a cloud of smoke. She was a chain smoker who went through two to three packs of cigarettes every day. At times, she'd have two cigarettes lit at once, having forgotten that she had one going in a different room.

"Puff, puff, puff that cancer stick. Puff, puff, puff, until it makes you deathly sick." It was a song I'd often sing just to irritate her.

"Shut the hell up." She scowled back, aggravated that I was right, yet pleased because she knew I cared and that was my way of showing it.

So I couldn't resist singing the verse a couple more times before going back to watching TV and leaving my mom to smoke her cigarette butts and read her romance novel in peace.

About an hour later she hurried into the living room and started bundling up in layers of clothes and putting on work boots.

"*Now* what are you doing?" I questioned.

"The little store is open, and I need to get cigarettes."

There was a small neighborhood grocery store about a half mile from our home. The people who owned it lived next door to their business so they were often open even in bad weather. But this blizzard was more than bad, it was dangerous.

"Are you crazy?" I asked. "They won't find your body until the snow melts in the spring."

She didn't say a word as she finished piling on mittens, scarves, and hats then trudged off into this raging blizzard. I shook my head and went back to watching my television show, convinced that was the last time I'd see her alive. I could have protested, but it would have done no good. When my mom needed a smoke, that was it. I figured there was no reason for two of us to get lost in a blizzard.

An hour and a half later the door rattled and in she came, covered in snow and toting a grocery sack with seven cartons of cigarettes. After this incident of almost having to go without her smokes, she always kept a few packs of cigarettes hidden in the drop ceiling of our kitchen. The haunting part of the whole situation is that my taunting song became a reality many years later when her addiction finally made her deathly sick.

Coward

I had many dogs over the years, but Princess, a beautiful black lab, was the most determined hunter. I considered her my dog because I'd been the one allowed to pick her out from a batch of puppies. My mom took me to the house of a man who had a litter of pups he was anxious to sell at the reduced price of twenty-five dollars. The dogs were in a kennel run attached to the garage. I sat cross-legged on the floor of the garage near the side door, and waited until he released a litter of eight puppies that burst forth tumbling and scurrying across the floor. The smallest puppy kept hopping into the air and chasing the other pups around, nipping their tails. I liked her spunk immediately. When this little pup climbed onto my lap twice, I knew she was the one. She was frisky and unafraid. We'd previously had a dog named Queenie whom I adored. My dad got rid of her after she bit the heads off of some of our baby pigs.

"That dog's ruined. She'll be bloodthirsty now," he'd said and took her to the dog pound.

In Queenie's honor, I gave this dog another royal name, Princess. On her registrations papers, my mom wrote *Phil's Midnight Princess* as her registered name. It was with Princess that I honed my dog training skills. Her training became a passion for me and had the added benefit of being a distraction from the chaos always brewing inside my house.

I repeated a routine I developed on my own until she'd mastered what I wanted her to learn. I'd give Princess the command to fetch. When she returned with the retrieving dummy or stick, I'd kneel down, look right in her eyes, and praise her. The words of Miss Jasper, my P.E. teacher, stuck in my head. *Good job, Phil. Keep up the hard work.* These were the words that made me try even harder so I used the same strategy with Princess.

"Good dog, Princess. You did a good job. What a great dog you are." I lavished her with praise following a nice retrieve.

If she ran off with the dummy instead of bringing it right back, I'd shake my finger at her, change the tone of my voice to one of disappointment, and scold her. She would hang her head. We spent every weekend and each day after school doing this, and we both looked forward to this time together. Soon, she was not only retrieving but had also learned to shake, sit, stay, and lie down. We all loved Princess, everyone but my dad. Not surprisingly, he carried not only a mean streak for our family but unleashed his cruelty onto our dogs as well.

"You want to know how to train a dog the right way? This is how you train an animal," he claimed, puffing out his chest.

I cringed and felt suddenly sick to my stomach recalling the way he used to beat and kick our beloved Labrador Trixie, who'd been my companion until she just took off one day when I was seven and never returned home. My dad had pinched Trixie's ears with a pair of pliers on many occasions until her ears had bled. Not being able to stand her yelps of pain, I had run inside many times and hid in my room with my hands covering my ears, wishing I could do the same thing back to him. Each time, I'd wait for him to leave then clean Trixie's wounds and smear bag balm cream on her tender ears. Trixie was never mean in return and never bit or snarled during one of his beatings. She just took it. I still wonder what happened to her and if it was my dad who drove her away.

This day, however, he'd burst out of the back door clutching a pair of pliers and demanding I bring him Princess. I hoped against all odds that he was going to set the pliers down, intending to use them to fix something around the yard later on. At nine months old, Princess was almost completely trained, which was not bad since I was only ten years old and was proud of her confidence and skill. I swallowed hard and slowly led Princess over to him. He grabbed her by the collar and jerked my proud, loyal dog right up next to him and commanded her to sit. When Princess obeyed and sat patiently, a look of disappointment crossed my dad's face.

"Give me that retrieving dummy!" he ordered next. He heaved it forty feet into the yard and waited for Princess to retrieve it.

She sprinted at top speed, snatched the dummy, and then brought it proudly back to me instead of my dad. My dad's face turned red, and he let out a string of cuss words as if he'd been personally insulted by this horrible offense of Princess's. He booted her in the rear and yelled,

"That damn dog needs to know who is giving the commands around here."

He grabbed her harshly by the collar and dragged her to the same spot, but this time Princess refused to fetch. Her eyes ping-ponged between my dad and me, her body drooped, and she turned a few confused circles, but she did not tuck her tail. My heart soared at her bravery. No one dared to buck my dad. Then the glint of metal flashed in front of me, and in an instant Princess's ear was clamped tightly between the pliers. But this wasn't Trixie. Princess lurched away, turned, and sunk her teeth into his hand, snarling. My dad dropped the pliers and pulled his bleeding hand away, cursing. He pulled a handkerchief from his back pocket, which he quickly wound around his fingers. The clean cloth soon turned crimson. I was elated and frightened at the same time.

"I'll shoot that damn dog," he shouted as he stormed into the house.

"Let's go," I called to Princess, and we headed toward the fields about half a mile from Norton-Froehlich. Princess and I wove our way through bushes and tree lines for the rest of the afternoon. She was unaware of what was waiting for her at home and raced after squirrels and rabbits with a carefree heart. I was crushed with worry. When dark set in, we headed off for home and took the route back that gave me a clear view of our house from a distance. My dad's pickup was gone. He didn't return home for two days.

All the next week I kept Princess away from him, spiriting her away, taking her with me when I ventured outside. I tried to catch a glimpse of the injured hand yet worried that if I got too close to him, I might be a reminder of what had transpired out in the yard last weekend. I slept fitfully all week, sensing a strange undercurrent to my dad's mood. Surprisingly, the next week the incident just blew over and was soon forgotten. I was so proud of Princess. She had defended herself against the raging brute whom I considered all-powerful and invincible. For the first time, I was able to see the many cracks in his false armor. It only defended him against those who were weaker, female, or who didn't fight back. I dared to let a new thought creep into my head. *Maybe someday I'll be strong enough to protect all of us.*

****

Several months later I was sitting in the passenger's seat of the pickup next to my dad, driving down the main road leading out of the Norton section. A man standing along the road gave a curt nod and motioned for my dad to pull over. My dad gave a friendly wave and pulled the pickup over to the side of the road. The man stepped toward the driver's side. My dad could be polite, charming, and good-natured when it benefited him, which is how he got away with being an abuser behind closed doors. I kept the abuse quiet because I didn't think anyone would believe what he was really like. He greeted the man in the same warm way he did every acquaintance.

"Hey, Joe. Where's my money for the stud service on that horse?" the man asked.

My dad shook his head. "Cash wasn't part of the deal."

"You crooked son-of-a-bitch!" The man took a step forward and punched my dad through the open window.

My dad's look changed instantly and his eyes filled with fear. He frantically shifted the pickup into drive and tore down the road. I sat wordlessly wondering if he would stop down the road a ways and go back to fight the guy. I thought of the many times he'd told me to go back and stand up for myself or called someone a yellow-belly for not fighting. He just kept on driving, his eyes as big as saucers.

The incident was never talked about again, but the cracks in his armor had deepened further. To a child, it was confusing. He evoked fear in my family yet seemed well-liked by almost everyone we met. He encouraged me to solve problems with other kids by fist fighting, yet I'd never seen him do the same except with members of our own family. This man who delighted in flaunting his power had sat silently next to me, arms stiff, eyes straight ahead, mouth pulled tight. I vowed I would never run from a fight.

The Bad Santa

Ha ha ha ha ha!

I was walking past the boys' restroom at Axtell Park Junior High when I heard this howling laughter spilling into the hallway. The commotion got my attention so I peeked my head inside the door and saw seven guys standing in a semicircle. There in the center was Curtis Leroy Ager demonstrating one of his many unique talents. Curt was indeed a unique individual. At fifteen years old he stood 6'1" and weighed 180 pounds. This gift of early maturity was a coveted asset in a rough junior high where many differences were settled in the hallways or after school using fists. I was a 100-pound ninth grader and for protection, sometimes gravitated toward those who had admirably matured early.

Like many of us, Curt had an assortment of homemade tattoos. The jailhouse tattoos, as they were sometimes called, were made by dipping a needle into India ink then poking the ink into the skin over and over, hundreds of times, until the dotted line extended into the desired shape, usually a cross, heart, or the person's name. One can only imagine the quality of these uneven and disproportioned designs that resulted from the hands of unskilled junior high kids. Curt was covered with these tattoos. "HATE" was tattooed on one hand, one letter on each knuckle of the four fingers. "LOVE" was tattooed on the other hand.

"HATE is the hand I punch people with, and LOVE is the hand I use on my girl," he'd explained, bringing a smile to our faces just as he was doing again today.

"Okay. Here it is again," Curt told his audience.

A hush fell across the room, and I looked on in amusement as a stream of urine shot clear up into the air and splashed off the ceiling. Our whoops of laughter filled the air, and we never thought to consider what the custodial staff had to clean up.

"The trick is to pinch the tip of your bad boy to build up pressure, then let it fly! The Sioux Falls Fire Department should hire me!"

Curt seemed to have everything going for him. In addition to being funny, likeable, inked, and mature, he was a superb athlete. At the spring all-city track meet, I followed a crowd over to watch Curt demonstrate his unusual method of high jumping. He was so tall and lanky that he could jump like a deer over the crossbar. He did not Fosbury Flop or scissor jump; he ran and hurdled the high jump bar exactly the same way hurdlers did in a race.

"I got my practice running through backyards and leaping over fences to get away from cops," he explained to the adoring onlookers.

The bar was set at five feet six inches. Only two jumpers remained—a kid from Patrick Henry Junior High and Curt. The other kid missed, knocking the cross bar off. It was up to Curt. All he had to do was clear the bar and he'd be city champion. A dozen of us stood on the side cheering him on while he warmed up for the last jump. Curt had never cleared this height previously. He backed up fifteen yards, sprinted, and leaped in his typical hurdle fashion right over the bar with a good inch to spare. He was so pumped that he went on to win the long jump event as well by leaping over nineteen feet.

Home was unpredictable. So school was home. Curt's favorite subject was history, and the teacher, Mr. Spars, often took the class on outings. Mr. Spars didn't do this for every class, only that one for some reason. It was the seventies, so unlike current times, Mr. Spars wasn't held to a rigid pacing guide that dictated his daily lessons. He was able to build relationships, take his class on picnics to the park by the zoo, and long after Curt had forgotten how to diagram a sentence he still remembered the teacher who cared about him.

There were signs of trouble, though. Sometimes I arrived at school to find that Curt had slept in the back of his car in the school parking lot. He'd had a fight with his stepdad and gotten kicked out of the house for a while. When this happened he'd try parking in the lot next to the zoo, but the police often came around in the middle of the night and made him move on so he'd drive over to Axtell Park. On those days, Curt would go inside the school as soon as it opened and shower in the locker room. He started skipping school whenever he got the chance to do an odd job and earn money. From there, things spiraled out of control. He and a friend started stealing motorcycles out of a fenced area attached to a repair shop. One person climbed the fence while the other stayed outside and curled the bottom of the fence up. The person on the inside tipped the motorcycle on its side and slid it under the fence. They'd ride the motorcycles until the engines stalled, and then dump them in Sandy Creek behind the school. Eventually, they got caught and Curt was slapped with probation. This led to another family fight after which he soon found himself kicked out of the house for good just after turning sixteen. He tried to stay in high school, but his time was consumed with earning enough money for food and finding a place to stay.

Winter temperatures dip well below freezing for several months out of the year in South Dakota, and Curt was living out of his car. He slept on the backseat and kept a cardboard box with his few clothes and possessions on the front seat. Finding a warm place to stay was a constant battle. He didn't lose his passion for life but remained upbeat and sociable so was often able to find a friend to stay with for a few days here and there. Because he bounced around to so many places, he got in the habit of carrying a black permanent marker with him and writing his name on everything, and I mean *everything*. He wanted to be able to prove what was his. Whether it was his or not. When he didn't have a friend to stay with, a lounge chair by the indoor pool at the Holiday Inn served as a warm place to sleep until security kicked him out.

Curt rarely seemed down. He hadn't lost his knack for squeezing the zest out of life. Although his car was one of his only possessions, he used to enter it in street stock races at Huset's Speedway on weekends. For safety reasons, cars couldn't contain any glass so he removed all the windows, then cut a piece of plexiglass to fit the front windshield which he taped in when he wasn't racing to make the car street-legal. He'd also have to tape the headlights and taillights back in after racing.

This fast-paced lifestyle didn't end on the racetrack. Curt went through many, many girlfriends. One of his teenage girlfriends regularly snuck out her bedroom window late at night to hang out with us. Her dad found out about her nightly adventures with this bunch of tattooed hooligans but wasn't able to convince her to stay away from us. His solution? He went to the hardware store, bought a length of chain and two padlocks, and physically chained her to the bed at night with one end of the chain padlocked around her ankle and the other around the bedpost. Word got out, though, and the police showed up at the girl's house. They told her dad he couldn't shackle her, and he had to give them the chain and padlocks. I guess her dad recognized we weren't good influences.

Curt finally acquired a nickname a few years later. He was invited to a get-together at someone's house around Christmas. People left the room, and when they came back Curt was gone as were several packages from under the tree. He had stolen some presents for himself. He later told me he didn't think they needed all those Christmas presents just for themselves. Curt hadn't had good Christmases growing up, so he took it upon himself to provide his own Christmas that year at the expense of others. So, we started calling him the Bad Santa, the St. Nick who takes instead of gives. He confirmed his nickname a few years later when he struck again. He'd given his girlfriend some presents that were wrapped and under her tree. After they had broken up one evening, he went in and took back all the presents. A true Grinch indeed. He struck a third time just before Christmas when he was low on cash and needed a gift for his mom. He went back to the indoor pool at the Holiday Inn, took two lounge chairs and two ashtrays, and headed to his mom's house armed with his newly acquired gifts. He didn't always wait for Christmas to pinch gifts. Years later, just days before I was to be married, I was having lunch at Burger King with the Bad Santa and just before we left, he grabbed a set of salt and pepper shakers and presented them to me in the parking lot.

"Here, Phil. You and your wife will need these for your new home." I still have that special gift from the Bad Santa.

I always believed he would make a great case study for anyone going into child psychiatry.

Fighting Back

Over the years, I noticed changes in my mom. She became less optimistic and more irritable. Her requests to be taken out on dates by my dad trickled, then suddenly stopped. She seemed to have resigned herself to a lifetime of disappointment and lies. Late one Saturday night my mom drove me to the Rainbow Bar, a place my dad often went to get drunk. She sent me in to find him. I shuffled through the bar with my head down until I found my dad sitting in a back booth with some drunken woman who was hugging and kissing on him. It embarrassed me, and my stomach wrenched at the sight. When I got back to the car, I told my mom he wasn't in the club. She knew what he was doing, though. She protected herself from all this betrayal by throwing herself into her work, both to support her family and to avoid problems at home. She had quiet ways of fighting back, too.

My mom often warned us of the dangers that could result from our heating unit. Crazy Clay, a guy who lived not far from us, died when his furnace exploded. It blew the house up and slightly sideways on the foundation. Tales of what happened filled the neighborhood. Some kids said that when Clay was brought out of the house, his hair was burned off, and he was purple from the concussion. I just remember the windows being blown out and the house sitting crooked until it was torn down. Wanda Wulff, who lived in the Froehlich section, said a home exploded near her place one morning while she was getting ready for school. The explosion rattled the house, knocking pictures off the wall. A heating specialist explained that the culprit was liquid propane. Also, the pilot light switches weren't as good back then, and even professionals got killed working on these old heating systems. Since then, many cities have banned individual propane tanks from being next to homes.

"Get in the car. The pilot light went out, and your dad's going to relight it," my mom said, grabbing her purse.

"Again?" I asked. I didn't remember the pilot light going out in past years, but now it had happened twice in two months.

We got in the car, and my mom backed out of the driveway until she reached the spot just down the street where we'd waited the last time. My mom sat rigidly. She was smoking a cigarette and nervously biting at her lip. When my dad finally appeared on the front steps to motion us in, I thought I saw her face fall. Something didn't seem right.

Years later when I asked my mom why she took so much crap from my dad without doing something about it, she scrunched up her face in anger.

"How many times when you kids were away at your aunt's and uncle's, do you suppose our pilot light went out? Your dad had to relight the furnace many times. So, I was trying to do something about him." She leaned in closer to me, her eyes on fire by now. "And why do you think I told you not to move toys off the front step? All those times he came home drunk and in the dark, and not once did he trip on something and hit his head!"

When I was younger, my mom had often told me to quit moving things off the front step. She'd say that if she put something there, it was for a reason. It seemed like a bad idea, though. Someone could trip, I'd think. Turns out, she was thinking the same thing. So, in her own way she was fighting back by setting out toys and snuffing out the pilot light, hoping to increase the chance that my dad would hit his head or get blown up.

PART TWO

THE DARKEST ROADS

Proverbs 25:26

Like a muddied spring or a polluted fountain is a man who gives way before the wicked.

Violence and Fear

Violence was all around me, and it seemed like a normal element of childhood. My dad ruled with fear and a heavy hand. Kids in the neighborhood and at school learned how to hit below the belt at an early age. Many of us were eager to fist fight at the slightest provocation. Even girls joined in these hostile, bloody fights. At school, a girl pounded another girl's head off the cement repeatedly until the girl was unconscious.

"Here's a souvenir of the fight for you," my friend laughed, tossing something from the ground at me after one particularly vicious girl fight.

I jumped back to avoid getting hit with a bundle of blonde strands and noticed the sidewalk littered with clumps of hair. At Axtell Park Junior High, twice I watched girls fight in just bras after getting their shirts ripped completely off.

The sixties and early seventies were filled with turmoil. News stations televised bloody scenes from Vietnam nightly. Cops were busting heads and turning dogs loose on war protesters and civil rights marchers. JFK, Bobby Kennedy, and Dr. Martin Luther King, Jr. were blown away. The Black Panthers and anti-government groups like the Symbionese Liberation Army gathered together and promoted their violent ways. By the time I was fifteen, I knew five teenagers who were homicide victims. So violence was all around me and, as a result, I took on a violent attitude.

Even the sport of wrestling, in which I excelled, encompasses the thrill of aggression and adversity. We had frequent fistfights in the practice room. During one hostile practice match, I went in for a takedown, and my wrestling partner kneed me in the face, breaking my nose. That was the first time it was broken. The second time was when a wrestling partner threw an elbow. This controlled fighting was a good outlet for my anger, yet it never completely erased my rage which still simmered below the surface.

Even God didn't seem capable of escaping the violence. Messiah Lutheran Church sat between the Norton and Froehlich sections of my neighborhood. One night, someone threw a firebomb known as a Molotov cocktail through the stained glass window. The church was closed down for a long time until funds were raised to replace the burned-out sanctuary.

Violence, anger, and hate spiraled around me, and I responded by acting out in aggressive ways. Because of this, I dealt with many fears when I was younger. As a child, I feared my dad, bullies, certain kids at school, and even walking past abandoned houses in the neighborhood at night made me on edge. An instinct for self-preservation kicked in, and I searched for ways to control these fears. I avoided many people. I banded together with friends for mutual protection. As I matured, I honed my skills as both a wrestler and street fighter, and things began to change for me. I began lifting weights regularly and became strong and muscular. Eventually, my fear of people began fading away, and was replaced with the confidence that now I was the one to be feared. I'd gone to the other extreme. I was in a position to not take crap from anyone. My buddies were tough as nails and ready to fight in an instant. Life was good.

Birds of a Feather

I love you. These simple words carry with them the power to develop emotionally healthy children. While growing up, I *never* heard these words spoken to me. My mom and dad never said this. My sisters and I never said these words to each other, nor did my grandparents or other relatives utter them. I still wonder why no one said such an important phrase. Growing up, my basic needs for food, shelter, and clothing were fulfilled for the most part, unless my dad blew a bunch of money. So I was often told, "Actions speak louder than words. I show you I love you." But my parents didn't hesitate to expose me to bickering and hostility. There didn't seem to be much to balance the fighting and the harsh circumstances of the neighborhood. Unsupervised and running the streets, I began to hang out with other kids who yearned for close family relationships. When I was older, the promise of a substitute family unit drew me to a dubious peer group.

At 6'1" and 215 pounds, my good friend Matt Lofton could turn dangerous in a split second. Before his reign of crime was complete, he had a rap sheet of forty-two arrests and served four stretches in the South Dakota State Penitentiary. The best way to describe Matt was out of control. He had spent part of his early life near the projects in Chicago around people who stole, lied, and manipulated, which caused him to adopt a take-what-you-want-from-the-world mentality as well. Matt despised cops and would fight them or elude them on foot or by car in an instant, feeling that they were just out to get him. I was riding with Matt one night when he outran or actually outmaneuvered a cop. This was a stunt that had served him well more than once. Matt was a "gear head" and usually had an enviably fast car. To get away, he would race down a street at speeds close to 100 mph to put distance between him and the patrol car. He'd slam on the brakes and get around a corner until he was out of sight. Then he'd quickly pull his car up in a driveway behind a hedge or right into someone's backyard and turn off his headlights. As soon as the cop flew by trying to locate him, Matt would back out and head in the direction from where the pursuit originated. The trick worked, yet with forty-two arrests, the cops were winning this game. Even as out of control as Matt was, if a friend needed help in any way, he'd be right there.

Doug Wallin acquired the nickname "Mr. I.," which stood for Mr. Irritable, due to his quick, hostile temper. It made him a good person to have on your side when a confrontation popped up. He stood 6'2" and weighed 235 pounds, and when he said something he always meant it. Always. If you got on his wrong side, he'd hold a grudge forever, and he'd never forget a face. When we were in our early twenties, I was in a grocery store with Doug picking up something for supper. I was talking away and noticed his face suddenly changed from Doug to Mr. I. He had a hard stare, and it was as if he no longer heard what I was saying.

"What's wrong with you?" I asked, looking to see what he was seeing.

Mr. I. didn't say a word. He strode up to a man looking at the canned soup and kicked the guy in the butt so hard that he crumpled to his knees.

"What the...?" The guy stood and faced Doug.

"Remember me? I'm Doug Wallin. I told you in high school that if I ever saw you again I'd kick your ass, and now I just did. If you want any more trouble, we can take it outside."

"You're crazy," the guy said and walked away.

Another friend, Wilbur, was an athletic 6'0" and 190 pounds. He wasn't much of a fighter in his late teens. After running with us, though, he became one of the fiercest street fighters I ever knew. He only wants to be known as Wilbur.

At 5'9", I had grown into a muscular, 200-pound frame and had not only been in many street fights growing up but had spent hundreds of hours learning how to attack my opponents and counter moves on the wrestling mat. Wrestling is similar in many ways to an organized fight, and all my years of training made me the most efficient street fighter out of all of us.

Our personalities melded into a notorious group for a town our size. Once we started down the dark road, we didn't hesitate to brawl or back down from trouble. Our philosophy was that we weren't going to take any crap from anyone while we were out on the town. As long as people left us alone, fine. If someone wanted a problem, though, they had come to the right guys. Mr. I. often fired a verbal warning shot to someone harassing us by saying, "Look, you jerk. If you keep messing with us, I'm going to end up in jail tonight, I'll have to pay your dental and doctor bills, and I'll be on probation, but I guarantee you one thing: before I go to jail, I'll make *sure* it's worth my while." He delivered this in an even, no-nonsense tone along with eyes ablaze with rage. Most of the time, this squelched the problem, and the culprit—drunk, cocky, or both— would slink off quietly. But there were other people just as tough and violent out in the clubs, so this dark road was riddled with many pitfalls and traps just waiting to ensnare us.

Research shows that changes in the brain occur into the early twenties, and the frontal lobes which are responsible for reasoning and problem-solving develop last. The frontal lobes help squelch the craving for thrills and taking risks. Not surprisingly, we thought out our philosophy only as far as our noses, convinced we weren't doing anything wrong, only reacting to what others started. We knew what could happen that night but didn't really extend our worries beyond that. None of us really thought out the consequences *all* the way to the end. Also, none of us had anything in the way of money or possessions, so being sued didn't matter to us. Jail time? No big deal. The worst part about going to jail was missing out on a night of fun; there was no shame that followed something as trivial as getting tossed in the slammer once in a while. Fired from a job? Just go get a different one. My dad was out of the picture, and my mom was rarely around as she worked two jobs. But when she did come to bail me out of jail, she'd yell at the cops and make it all their fault. So, there was not much in the way to deter our wild lifestyle. We were in the fast lane speeding down the dark roads of life with some pretty dim headlights.

Here I am pounding iron in the gym, so that I was prepared to pound people in the streets.

Here is the Bad Santa living life in the fast lane.

Standing: Leonard Sorensen (Hat Man), Matt Lofton, Doug Wallin (Mr. I.), me, Curt Ager (the Bad Santa), Wilbur. Seated: Dan Lofton, who was paralyzed in a devastating vehicle accident following a wild night.

Foreshadowing Eyes

Have you ever seen eyes that bored a hole right through you, turning your blood cold? I'm not referring to your everyday angry eyes or even eyes that burn with fire; those I regularly saw during fights and wrestling matches. Deadly eyes are the ones that change in a split second from normal eyes to ones that spell imminent danger.

Benny was a bad dude who went to my junior high, but dropped out before high school. I saw him around town once in a while. When I was a junior, some guys from school organized a huge keg party out in the country. Parties like this were regular events around Sioux Falls. Many kids would spread the word about the party's whereabouts, which was usually in a farm field or by the river outside the city limits. There were around 300 kids milling about in an open area by the Big Sioux River, throwing back cold beers from one of the many sixteen-gallon kegs and listening to a local rock band. I was standing near a cluster of parked cars when Benny and a couple of his tough friends pulled up. Benny had a longstanding reputation as a fearless and merciless fistfighter whose eyes could turn deadly in a second if someone crossed him. He drove past the parked cars, backed up to one of the kegs, and all three slowly got out of the car.

"You have a lot of beer. We want this keg." Benny never said much. He didn't need to. A hush fell over the growing ring of people surrounding the keg while Benny just stood there with those cold eyes, scanning the crowd with the quiet confidence that assumed not one of the hundreds of people in attendance would challenge him. He was right, of course. There were football players, wrestlers, and college guys, but no one who wanted to risk a night in the hospital over a keg. Benny and his friends loaded up the keg and drove back off into the night, their taillights soon fading to a dim blink while the party-goers started back up their buzz of conversations.

Two years later, Benny joined the military. He was home on leave and was going through some personal problems so made the decision he didn't want to go back. He took a high-powered rifle and shot himself in the calf with the intention to just wound himself enough so that he wouldn't have to return to the military. The muzzle velocity was much more powerful than he'd anticipated, and he ended up blowing his lower leg nearly off resulting in amputation at the knee. In spite of this, he went on to get in many brawls and remained a dauntless fighter. Benny was good to me even though he was older. He and his friends came to watch me wrestle a few times, and he even took me out with his buddies, which made me feel like I'd been chosen for a special group since he was selective about his companions. He was a hard guy who lived a hard life, and this eventually caught up with him. He didn't live to see fifty.

Eyes can tell a lot about a person, not just whether the person is about to lose his cool. Eyes can tell other stories, and I've always had a knack for noticing eyes. Perhaps this attention to detail comes from my interest in art. Growing up, I won ribbons for drawings I'd done. I made a foretelling comment to a friend one day that has stuck with me all these years.

"There's something disturbing about her eyes," I whispered, nodding toward the girl across the room, a mutual friend of ours. My friend shrugged. I couldn't quite explain it, but she just carried herself differently, her shoulders hung, and her eyes didn't trust anybody.

"I'll make you a bet. She'll end up being on drugs or an alcoholic." And she did and still is to this day. Even before reaching adulthood I saw many eyes that said *I will live with a man who abuses me forever.* Those eyes reflected a self-esteem beaten so low that the person behind them could never reach her potential. It came from being subjected to verbal, physical, or sexual abuse, and the despair showed through the windows of their eyes.

Protection from Above

Wilbur was one of the fiercest, most aggressive street fighters around town during our heyday, but he wasn't always that way. When Mr. I., Matt, and I were twenty-one and hanging in rough clubs, Wilbur was only eighteen. We developed a method to get him into clubs even though he was underage. We kept a set of red, black, blue, and green felt-tip pens in the vehicle. The three of us who were of legal age went into the club while Wilbur waited in the car. We'd show our IDs and get stamps on our hands, which let anyone working the club know we'd been carded. A few minutes later I'd go back out to the car and use the appropriately colored felt-tip pen to draw the stamp design onto Wilbur's hand. I'm a pretty good artist, so when Wilbur walked back to the club with me, he'd show the bouncer the fake stamp on his hand. It was never questioned.

During this period of our lives, we were in many fistfights, and being younger than us, Wilbur would stand back wide-eyed while the fists flew. I would get angry and yell at Wilbur.

"Why the hell don't you grow some balls and fight with us?"

We were not good influences and within a year, Wilbur was fighting right alongside us every time. His transformation into a fighter happened quickly and unexpectedly. I had taken Wilbur out with me to some clubs one winter night, and at about 2:30 A.M. we went back to the apartment that Wilbur shared with Mr. I. I was standing on the sidewalk pitching snowballs to Wilbur, who was hitting them with an old bat. A car drove by us and one of the occupants yelled, "Hey, you asses! Get inside!" I whipped the snowball I had already in my hand and made a great shot, hitting the car with loud smack. Almost instantly the car's brake lights went on, and the car pulled a slow U-turn.

"Hey, Wilbur, here we go. Are you ready to fight?"

Wilbur didn't say anything. The car pulled up close to us and came to a stop. Car doors slammed, and two big, tall men came walking toward us, quickly closing the gap between their car and where we stood. They appeared to be in their late twenties and looked rough.

"I'll smash your face," one of the guys said while walking toward Wilbur.

Wilbur raised the baseball bat in a threatening manner and the guy stepped back, raising his hands for protection. But then he turned to his buddy and said, "Willy, get my piece from under the seat."

My heart jumped into my throat, as Willy ran back toward their vehicle. *We're going to get shot!* I was just ready to bolt off running when from somewhere above me I heard, "Don't even think about reaching into that car unless you want your head blown off." It was Mr. I. From inside the apartment, he had heard the commotion and had come onto the roof of the porch through a big old window. He was kneeling on one knee and staring down the barrel of a twelve-gauge shotgun which was now pointed at Willy, who stood near the vehicle. Willy froze in place then slowly backed away from the car. It was freezing out and Mr. I., clad only in underwear and a pair of boots, added to the bizarre nature of the whole scene playing out beneath the glow of a single streetlight.

"You dudes stopped for a fight, so you better believe you'll get one," Mr. I. yelled without lowering the gun. He said it with the same conviction he'd demonstrated time and time again over the years. He shouted to Wilbur, "Put the bat down and fight that guy."

The instant Wilbur dropped the bat the guy closest to him blasted Wilbur with a devastating punch to the face. I squared off with Willy, and my first punch got him right on the bridge of his nose, actually busting his glasses into pieces. Next I switched into wrestling mode and shot in low with a double leg take-down that lifted him off his feet and slammed him onto his back. When I took him down, we both hit the street, and a big piece of skin tore off the back of my hand. Willy wasn't a fighter, and I beat the spunk out of him easily. He was on his back and didn't move from the street. I stood to see Wilbur still brawling with the other guy. They exchanged punches evenly for several minutes when the guy's endurance ran out. Wilbur didn't hesitate. He was on top of the guy in a flash, pounding the back of his head repeatedly on the cement while the man tried to grasp at Wilbur to lessen the impact. I finally stopped Wilbur, who was in a violent frenzy. Mr. I., still clad only in underwear and standing on the roof of the porch with the stock of the shotgun resting on his hip, yelled down.

"Hey, you two creeps wanted to be tough guys, but you found out you're not so bad ass. In fact, you just took a pounding from guys ten years younger. Get the hell out of here, and don't ever come back."

They retreated to their car silently, and I heard Willy say, "Man, where are my glasses?"

I spotted the remains of his glasses on the street and handed the three pieces to Willy. "Here you go, man," I said to this dude who couldn't even land one punch in a fight.

I was thankful Mr. I. was a light sleeper who kept a shotgun near his bed. After that incident, Wilbur never hesitated to fist fight, and I don't recall him ever losing a brawl.

Tempting the Grim Reaper

We slipped out of dangerous situations with a regularity that paralleled the way most people slip out of a pair of shoes without giving it a second thought. When you live in the fast lane and are running out of control, you survive by sheer luck or by the help of guardian angels. Firearms, fighting, felonies, fast women, and fast vehicles all came into the mix.

Without meaning to, we had a knack for unintentionally making everyday decisions just a little more dangerous: hanging in the roughest parts of town, frequenting the rowdiest clubs, and riding motorcycles recklessly, of course without a helmet. I was in a few accidents on my motorcycle where I ended up flying through the air like a rag doll and scraping my limbs but walking away with my brains still inside my head. One thing I had in my favor was that I was never a speed freak. It just wasn't my thing, but it was for plenty of my friends so I literally went along for the ride with them. Matt had a souped-up Mustang built from the bottom up for speed with the pistons and cam all the way down to a Dana rear end. In the upper corner of the front windshield, he'd painted the number 13.3 indicating his fastest quarter-mile time at Thunder Valley Speedway where he'd gone to be timed. It was a fast quarter-mile time because cars were heavier then since they weren't made out of the lighter materials that comprise modern cars. He often drove that car 60 to 70 mph in town and over 100 mph on two-lane highways outside of town. We had more than one close call in that street-legal rocket ship.

Matt was at the wheel of his mom's 1967 Valiant, and we were cruising south on Main Avenue just after dusk on a Friday evening. The pool tables would be swarming with college kids and other novice players, just ripe for the picking and a sure way to win enough money to last through the weekend. Still, we scoured the parking lots along the way, potential gathering spots for impromptu teen parties, to see if more exciting action was brewing along the street. I had just enough time to yell, "Oh no!" as a car barreled through a red light and rammed us broadside right on my door. There was a sickening crunch of metal and the shattering of glass punctuated by Matt's cursing. The vehicle spun around, and we skidded, finally ending up sideways in the street. Matt swore again and kicked open his door. By the time I'd crawled across the tangled mess of the front seat and exited through the driver's door, Matt was surveying the crumpled front end of the other vehicle, its radiator steam billowing skyward.

My legs were wobbly, and my body already ached. I felt drops of sweat dripping down my cheek, but when I went to wipe them away, I realized it was blood dripping from a gash on the side of my head. Then I saw the shards of glass and had to brush and shake them from my hair and clothes. It gave me a sick feeling remembering the time I was in a head-on collision, and I ended up bloody and covered in glass.

By now, the carload of teens who had run the red light and T-boned us were scurrying in and out of the car, all in various degrees of pain, but all focused on removing the beer from inside their smashed car to some bushes next to a brick building. They'd been drinking and still had a couple cases of beer with them. Filled with a combination of empathy for their bad decision-making and a distrust of the law, Matt and I actually helped them hide their beer. In the 1970s, there were no organizations or campaigns to spotlight the dangers of drinking and driving, so it generally warranted just a slap on the wrist unless you were underage. By the time the police arrived, the beer had disappeared from the car. The teen driver was ticketed for running a red light. Both cars were totaled.

Reunited with the Bad Santa

I was driving through downtown on my motorcycle at 1:00 A.M. The air was crisp, and I was headed for home after a night of shooting pool when I heard a voice shouting at me from a car.

"Hey, f*****, ready to go again?"

I glanced to my right and looking out the driver's side window at me was a guy from Hartford, South Dakota, whom I'd been in a fistfight with two months prior. There had been a big street dance going on in Hartford the evening of the fight, and I'd been shooting pool in a small bar on Main Street. We'd been playing for money when one accusation led to another and soon our fistfight had spilled onto the sidewalk outside the tavern. The guy had fought pretty hard, but the cops had shown up almost immediately, broken up the fight, and told me to leave town. As we'd parted ways the guy had threatened me by saying, "I'll see you again, and we'll finish this little ordeal."

So, now it was time to finish what we'd started eight weeks ago.

"Pull over into that lot, and I'll give you your second chance," I yelled back to him.

I turned my motorcycle into the parking lot, and as I came to a stop I saw about fifteen cars parked in the lot with a couple dozen people milling around or leaning on vehicles shooting the breeze on a Saturday night. This was a place where teens gathered to drink a beer or take a break from cruising the loop, and the cops didn't care unless they saw trouble, in which case they'd clear out the lot and send people on their way.

The Hartford guy had no sooner parked his car and stepped foot on the lot when we began to brawl. This guy was tough, and the fight rumbled on for some time. At one point, I lost my footing and fell to my knees. The guy didn't miss a beat. He kicked me in the face, busting my lips open. I stood quickly, sending spasms of pain through my head which only heightened my anger. My wrestling knowledge was a lifesaver, and I eventually took him to the ground after a long struggle. I held onto his hair and pounded his head on the concrete until all the fight was out of him. Exhausted and bleeding, I headed toward my motorcycle when I heard someone call my name.

"Phil! Nice fight, buddy!" It was the Bad Santa. I had to look up to see him. He still had the same wide grin and straggly hair but had grown to 6'3" and 240 pounds. He handed me a beer, and we stood by my cycle talking and catching up. I used the beer to keep washing the blood out of my mouth. As the night wore on, Curt told me how he was still struggling to make it in life. He didn't have a place to live but had started working a steady job again. As always, Curt was personable and eager to share some well-earned tales that left us both laughing at the way life can take such unexpected turns. The next day Curt moved in with me. I had another companion to accompany me down the dark roads.

A Damn Shame

Back in the seventies many nightclubs hired guys with reputations as fighters or big, intimidating football player types as bouncers rather than hiring trained security officers. It was generally known by the customers that if you started trouble in the bar, you'd likely get roughed up by the bouncers. As a bouncer, I usually worked with three or four other bouncers each night, which gave us the muscle to back each other up since periodically there were some big brawls that broke out involving drunken patrons. It usually went something like this: A recently legal age college kid grabs a waitress. The waitress complains to the bouncer. The bouncer tells the obnoxious intoxicated customer to leave. Intoxicated customer swears and refuses to budge. Bouncer grabs customer and begins hauling him to the door. Customer's friend jumps in and hits bouncer. Another bouncer shows up to help first bouncer. Another one of the customer's friends joins in until this domino effect erupts into a huge brawl. The most hair-raising times were when we found ourselves heavily outnumbered. In one of these mismatched fracases at the Macamba Club, I was looking around for backup when I saw our bartender get up onto the bar and jump like Spider-man onto a patron's back. The bartender wasn't a big guy, either, but thankfully was motivated for some reason to get involved in what was quickly becoming an out-of-control fight just before three cop cars pulled up.

Every club had a list of rules based on what commonly led to fights or what could lead to trouble during a fight. Generally the rules were no handguns, buck knives, or other weapons, no hats, no muscle shirts or tank tops, and no colors. This last rule could be especially problematic for bikers who did not appreciate having to remove their biker or gang colors. Sometimes they'd just say, "No, we're coming in," depending on how drunk they were, and then the bouncer would have to get right in front of them and stop their entrance. They might try saying, "I'm just gonna walk in and see if my buddy is here." One exceptionally drunk and obnoxious guy tried this line, and I when I stood in front of him to block his entrance, he pulled a knife out. When another bouncer showed up almost immediately, the guy got intimidated and put the knife away. We grabbed him, and he was arrested nonetheless.

Wilbur was bouncing in a club one night and working with him was a twenty-two-year-old college football player who was about 6'4" and 260 pounds. He was no one to mess with, and having some other big bouncers on your shift was always a welcomed relief. A scuffle broke out late that night between this football player and a customer. The football player had just slammed the guy to the floor when Wilbur came walking up to assist. Right as the football player reached down to grab the guy off the floor, the guy came up at him with a knife and stabbed the bouncer three times in the chest. The kid turned to face Wilbur, eyes wide with terror, and said, "I've been stabbed. I think I'm dying." He fell to the floor, and in desperation Wilbur pressed his hands against the surge of blood that was gushing out in a dark, almost black color. It was no use. One of the thrusts had hit the kid's heart, and he died right on the floor beneath Wilbur's hands. A good life lost over a stinking minimum wage job. Such a damn shame.

Grand Theft Joy Riding

I'd been glancing anxiously out the front window every time I walked past it waiting to see what sleek ride awaited me that night. I'd already cleaned everything in my little efficiency apartment and had started to straighten the only thing left, a row of wrestling medals hanging on a board in the living room. The medals represented skill rather than luck, which was important to me. I never counted on luck, choosing to rely on grueling training and intense desire to win instead.

A flash of light reflected off a medal and the roar of an engine outside announced my buddy Jim's arrival. Parked in front of the house was a 1970 fastback Mustang. It was fresh-from-the-car-lot shiny and pure red with chrome wheels that had probably cost a fortune, or at least more money than either of us had ever had to spend on something as non-functional as hubcaps. Jim Anderson carefully chose each car, taking into consideration the envy it would cause in friends and strangers alike, its ability to impress girls, and finally, but least importantly, its speed. Jim worked at a major car dealership in town that carried hundreds of cars, trucks, and four-wheelers. He had several jobs at the lot including driving vehicles from one sales lot to another and cleaning out the insides of the ones that were ready to be put out for sale. This gave him access to all the keys to every vehicle on the lot. Just before closing time, Jim would take the spare set of keys to whichever set of wheels suited his fancy for the night. After dark, he would drive his own car to the job site, park it, then take the dream ride for a spin. After our night of carousing was over, we'd put it back on the car lot, usually around 2:30 A.M., and Jim would replace the spare keys the next day at work. Slick. For over a year, it worked perfectly. We spent 1979 behind the wheel of more luxury cars than most people drive in a lifetime.

One night, the odds didn't roll in our favor. Frigid temperatures had settled in several weeks before freezing the city solid. The wind was howling and the night was dark, perfect weather for four-wheeling on the frozen Big Sioux River. So Jim took a four-wheel-drive Bronco from the lot for a fun-filled night of climbing snow-covered hills and trekking over the frozen river. We had just skidded down an embankment when Jim stepped on the accelerator and we cruised down the ice-packed river. We raced and slid for miles, bits of snow spraying behind the wheels and the headlights illuminating the endless smooth ice ahead, sometimes catching the movement of a small animal scampering back to the trees.

Without warning, the vehicle lurched, and I found myself thrown forward. My hands flew up reflexively to protect myself, but the force of the impact knocked my head against the dash and split my lip open. Blood started to pool in my mouth so I used the only thing I could find, my coat-sleeve, and wadded it against the gaping cut. Jim had been thrown into the steering wheel and held his head in his hands, swearing softly. Seatbelts had not yet gained much popularity, and I knew few people who ever wore one.

When we got our bearings we realized the front of the car was pointing down and we could see the headlights illuminating the swirling water. We'd broken through the ice and the rear of the car was slowly pointing skyward. Luckily, the river wasn't deep in this spot and the front of the Bronco soon came to rest somewhere on the bottom of the river and I found my hands tightly clenching the leather seat below me. Chunks of newly broken ice pattered against the hood, slowly approaching the side window. No way were we getting the vehicle out of that hole, and we were lucky we weren't further under water. There we sat stuck in the middle of the river on a moonless night, completely unprepared for being out in the elements. The temperature had continued to sink well below zero since we'd eaten our McDonald's hamburgers four hours ago. I was wearing a somewhat warm rust-colored nylon ski jacket, no gloves, and cowboy boots. The cowboy boots with their hard, sturdy heels were useful in a fight but rather useless for hiking through piles of snow in the howling wind. So we sat there and debated.

"How are we gonna get this vehicle out? I have to get it back to the lot," Jim said.

"Good luck with that! This vehicle isn't coming out of this hole. My biggest concern is how are we getting out of here."

"It's too cold to walk. We're too far down the river."

And then there was nothing else to say. So we sat some more until a tunnel of light appeared around the bend of the river, growing brighter as it approached. By an amazing stroke of luck, it was another vehicle out on the ice! I jumped out of the Bronco and flagged down the vehicle, steering them away from the thin ice. It was another vehicle full of teenagers out joy riding. We climbed in, they turned around, and we'd just started down the river when Jim spoke up.

"Hold on! I think I forgot something in my vehicle. I'll be right back." He climbed back out, disappeared inside the Bronco for a few minutes, and then returned. "Got it, thanks."

The teenagers drove us to a pay phone several miles away where we called Jim's brother to come and get us. That's when Jim told me he'd gone back to wipe the fingerprints off the steering wheel, shift lever, and the door handles inside and out. He'd waited until our rescuers had turned their four-wheeler around so they wouldn't wonder what he was doing.

We just left the Bronco where it was, and the next day Jim replaced the keys back at work. The car lot reported it stolen, and a few days later a farmer discovered the Bronco stuck in the ice. Subsequently, it was returned to the car lot and fixed up. The whole incident spooked us enough that we stopped taking weekend joy rides. We had to go back to trying to impress girls with my beat-up 1970 Ford pickup.

Bat Man and Beating the System

It was us against the world. That was our thinking, anyway. Rules were made for people who weren't clever enough to figure out a way around them. We did what we wanted, within reason of course, because the consequences didn't seem all that bad, maybe a night in jail followed by charges dismissed, probation, or paying restitution. Besides, we weren't stupid enough to get caught most of the time for much of what we were involved in. At the time, it struck us as more logical to try to outsmart the system rather than figure out a way to operate within the boundaries.

Early on, my friends and I came up with a slick process that allowed us to sidestep criminal charges following a brawl. After the dust had settled from our latest scuffle and the sun was rising on the collective welts, contusions, and fractures produced in the previous night's fight, we would check around to find out the names of the people we'd had the confrontation with. Then we'd go down to the police station and file charges against our rivals, making sure that the police report swung in our favor and pointed all blame at the other people. When the report arrived on the desk of the state's attorney, he would file charges against our rivals and thus, we had the state's attorney on our side. It was insult on top of injury for the defendants who then faced criminal charges following a butt-kicking on the streets.

We had to make the first move by filing a complaint against the others before they could file against us. Charges are probably filed differently today, but back then it worked. We didn't actually want anyone to end up with a record or jail time, not because we were nice guys, we just hated the courts more than we hated the guys we brawled with. So after the charges hung above their heads for a couple of weeks and the heat was off the incident, we'd call the state's attorney and ask to have the charges dropped. The call would go something like this:

"Mr. State's Attorney, we have decided to drop charges since things just got out of hand that night. We don't feel that we can testify against those folks."

Done deal. We had side-stepped criminal charges and didn't have to go into court to rat on people and get them in a legal bind. We just wanted to get our butts out of a jam—except for one time. Mr. I., Curt, and I were on our way to a house party in, of all places, Norton-Froehlich, when Curt came to a slow stop on the street just a couple houses down from the party.

"That S.O.B. needs to move his truck," Curt complained, clearly annoyed. The bright headlights from a pickup pierced the window of our car, and I squinted and shielded my eyes with one hand to get a better look. The pickup had pulled over into our lane and was sitting almost headlight to headlight with our vehicle on this narrow road. Curt leaned on the horn. The other driver rolled his window down and yelled, "F*** you. I'll kick your ass."

That was all the encouragement we needed. I bailed out my door and got a hold of the guy just as he stepped from his pickup. We swung around a few times, each trying to throw the other to the ground, when he tried to tackle my legs, and that was all I needed. I got him by the hair and tried to fling him to the ground, hoping to avoid wrestling on the street in the good clothes I'd just put on for the party. Where their head goes, their body follows in a fight, so I was hoping to throw him to the ground so I could give him the boots. By avoiding wrestling, I wouldn't get my clothes messed up or get scraped on the ground myself. He didn't go down, but I managed to pull his sweatshirt over his head and face. He was bent forward, and his arms had become tangled in the shirt. I held his shirt with one hand and delivered a few good punches to his nose with the other. I had control of this dude when I heard a *thud, thud, thud.* The Bad Santa had retrieved a baseball bat from the car and was pounding the guy across the back with some devastating blows. I immediately let go of the guy, and the Bad Santa whacked him again. When Curt stepped back, the driver managed to pull his shirt down and took off running down the street in his desperation to avoid bat man.

Mr. I. had joined us and said to Curt in his irritable voice, "Give me that bat." The air turned serious. You never knew about Mr. I. Part of me was half expecting Mr. I. to go after Curt with the bat the way he'd gone after him one time when Curt's dog had strewn garbage all over the apartment they shared. But instead Mr. I. proceeded to pound dents in the pickup, and just as I thought he was finished, he smashed the taillights and headlights for good measure. "That'll teach his ass a lesson about courteous driving and going around acting tough," Mr. I. said, his angry eyes illuminated by our vehicle's headlights.

By this time, people had gathered in the front yard of the party house, and one of the girls yelled down to us, "You're not allowed at this party. We saw what you did to Trevor and his pickup. We have your license plate number, and we already called the sheriff."

Great. These people knew the guy who'd just taken a beating. We split before the sheriff arrived on the scene, relieved that we'd gotten away in time and wouldn't have our Saturday night ruined by getting thrown in jail. At least we could finish our night out on the town. There was no way we could try to file charges on the other person with all the witnesses, so three days later, both Curt and I were arrested at my apartment and charged with assault, which included use of a deadly weapon. Mr. I. was never identified so he escaped charges. Someone at the party recognized me, and they'd gotten Curt's license number.

These were serious charges, and I told the Bad Santa we needed to do something to avoid going to trial. There was no way we could win in court. We put our heads together and decided to see what we could find out about Trevor. It turned out he didn't have a lot of money and lived in Norton-Froehlich. The Bad Santa went to his place and had a long talk with him. He explained it had been a fight that had gotten completely out of hand with both sides making hot-headed decisions beginning with Trevor initiating the whole ordeal.

"Look, Trevor, me and Phil will give you three hundred dollars each if you don't show up in court, and I have a connection to get your pickup fixed and repainted. Also, you won't be a rat to the courts." Bingo. Curt saw his eyes perk up with interest. Curt's mouth went dry waiting for his answer because bribing a state's witness could lead to more heavy-duty charges.

It took weeks before the court date arrived. The Bad Santa and I showed up a little early, sweating with worry that Trevor would come walking through the door at any minute. The judge called our names, and we walked to the front of the courtroom. The judge called Trevor's name. No one rose. He called his name two more times. Still nothing. We breathed a collective sigh of relief. Trevor had not shown.

"Your Honor, if the state can't provide a witness, why aren't these charges dismissed?" I asked.

The state's attorney approached the judge, and they whispered back and forth for a few moments. "Due to the seriousness of the charges, I'll delay this hearing for two weeks," the judge stated.

When Trevor failed to show for the second preliminary hearing, as well, all charges were dropped. Every criminal charge thrown at us was completely deserved, yet we viewed the courts as just another enemy to battle. The courts were just another obstacle to keep us oppressed so we justified using any means to win in court just like in a street fight. No rules, hit below the belt, and fight as dirty as possible to win.

Mr. Lofton . . . with the Pipe . . . in the Office

A tattered black woolen ski mask, a pair of black leather gloves, and a twelve-inch galvanized pipe wrapped with gray duct tape at one end. It was 10:00 P.M. on a Saturday, and I'd just stopped by my friend Matt's house where I was greeted by this sight spread out in a line on a table. They looked like pieces from the board game Clue, but they weren't intended for any game. Their mere presence was a signal to me that something devious was about to happen.

"Hey, what's with the pipe and ski mask?" I called to Matt, who was in the kitchen fixing himself something to eat.

"I'm going down to the trucking company to get that two thousand bucks from the desk drawer," he yelled back.

I cringed inside and went over to the doorway, where I stood rubbing my chin and already thinking of ways to counter what Matt had not yet said. I had worked for a trucking company in Sioux Falls but left the job over a year before for something with better hours. I frequently left one job for what appeared to be a better one. From the time I was fifteen until I was twenty-three, I'd burned through fifteen different jobs from food service to construction to the packing house and everything in between. One assignment at the trucking company on weekends was to hand out specific amounts of money to truckers who were going on the road. This was in the days before instant cash machines or debit cards so the truckers needed cash to pay for food or motel rooms. The company always kept this cash tucked inside a manila envelope and locked in the office desk drawer. Matt had decided this would be some easy money. The current weekend dispatcher was a retired man in his early seventies who was working to supplement his social security.

"Okay, so you're going to heist that two thousand bucks, but what's the pipe for?"

107

"I'll pop that old guy on the head and put him to sleep for five or ten minutes while I bust into the desk," Matt said matter-of-factly.

Matt, with an I.Q. of over 130, was generally the wisest and wittiest of us all but could turn uncharacteristically rash, irresponsible, and unrelenting when it came to criminal activity. One evening Matt had walked into a liquor store, quickly stashed a bottle of whiskey under his coat, paid for a bag of chips, and left. He always locked his car so no one would steal anything from *him*, so he had to set the bottle of whiskey on top of the car while he dug in his pocket for the keys. In the meantime, the bottle slid off the car and crashed on the ground. Matt cursed, bemoaning his bad luck and refusing to go in and buy a bottle after he'd gone to the trouble to steal one. So he went right back in, stole another bottle, and purchased a candy bar. His history of getting what he wanted had left me convinced this was another ill-considered idea. Frankly, I didn't care about the $2,000 being taken, but I knew Matt's plan wasn't going to play out as smoothly as it does in the movies when someone gets conked on the head and wakes up just fine a few minutes later.

"Come on, buddy, you'll put that old dude to sleep forever. You'll kill him," I reasoned with Matt.

"Nah, I won't hit the old guy that hard. Plus, I have the pipe taped on the end."

"Come on! Nobody can judge how hard to crack someone with a pipe to just knock him out. Let's come up with a plan for you to get that cash without killing the old dude."

I knew the old guy was the only person at the trucking company on a Saturday night, so I reasoned that if we could get him to leave the office area for a while Matt could bust into the desk and grab the cash. Matt would go down there with his ski mask and gloves on and hide under a semi in the parking lot just outside the office. At 11:15 P.M. I would call the trucking office. Matt would know the phone was ringing since the company had speakers in order for the phone to be heard throughout the complex. I would tell the old guy that I was an independent trucker and had left my personal tool box across the lot in the machine shop. I would tell the old guy to check for my tool box and bring it to the office, and I'd call him back in half an hour, after which I could drive down to the office to get my tools. This would get him out of the office for at least fifteen minutes since it was a long walk across the lot to search for a tool box that didn't exist. It would be plenty of time for Matt to break into the desk and snatch the manila envelope. Our plan was complete except for figuring out how Matt would break into the locked desk drawer.

"Take a crowbar and just bust the metal drawer open," I suggested.

"No, I'm going to take an electric drill," Matt reasoned, deciding that the drill fitted with a high-speed metal bit could bore the lock out quickly. He even had an extension cord attached to the drill. So Matt headed to the crime scene and against my advice took the twelve-inch duct-taped pipe for a backup. I didn't want Matt to kill the guy. Matt was like a brother to me, and I didn't want him to get the death penalty over $2,000. Something didn't feel right, and my mind replayed our plan over and over until the clock hand finally crept over to 11:15. I made my call from a pay phone several blocks from Matt's place. *Bringgg, bringgg.* The phone rang several times, and I sighed with relief when the old guy answered so I could get him out of the office.

"Hello. Trucking dispatch office," the voice on the other end said.

"Hey, buddy, I'm Bob Nelson, an independent trucker, and I left my personal tool box across in the machine shop. Will you go grab my tool box for me, and I'll call you back in thirty minutes to see if you found it? I'm almost positive I left it there, but I live way out of town and don't want to make the trip for nothing."

109

"Hell, no. I ain't walking across that lot. It's too damn cold out," the old guy snapped back irritably.

Crap. My stomach tightened. Matt was lying in wait with his pipe, and if the old guy didn't leave, I knew what would transpire. I had to think quickly.

"Come on, buddy. That tool box was a gift from my kids. I don't want some other trucker getting those tools." I spouted off the first line that popped into my head, not wanting to hesitate and give the guy time to think. I heard him mumbling curse words through the phone.

"Okay, damn it. Call me back at midnight." I heard a click, and the phone went dead.

My part was done, and I returned to Matt's place, where I now waited. And I waited, and I waited. The noise from the television was annoying me so I turned it off. Without the background noise, the silence of the house grew more constricting with every passing moment. There wasn't a sound inside or out. Forty minutes later the door swung open, and Matt stormed through the front door swearing and throwing his burglary gear onto the floor. I picked up the pipe and looked it over carefully for traces of blood. It was clean.

"What went down?" I yelled to Matt, but he didn't answer. Finally, he emerged from his room, still swearing to himself.

"Everything worked perfectly at first. I heard the phone ring, and through the office door I could hear that lazy old duffer complaining about the cold. Then he walked by me about a foot away while I was hiding under a semi cab. As soon as he left the building I went into the office, and the drill did its job. I drilled the lock right out, but the hooked tab attached to the lock kept the drawer from coming open. I should have used the crowbar like we talked about. I was waiting for him with my pipe when I heard him start talking to someone outside, so I left out the side door." Matt settled back into the couch shaking his head. Then he started laughing.

"What's so funny? You didn't get the cash, did you?"

"That lazy old codger. I should have done him a favor and hit him on the head. When he walked past me while I was hiding, he was talking to himself and swearing like a sailor because he had to walk across the lot."

So, Matt didn't get the money, and that old guy never knew how close he came to death or serious injury that night.

Bad to the Bone

During all our years of fighting, we ran into two types of tough guys: those who'd brawl hard until the fight was over, and those who transformed into a primitive blind rage. The latter would become so violent and aggressive during a fight that they were nearly impossible to stop. Mr. I. was the type of fighter who, on the few occasions when he was on the losing end, wouldn't quit until he was at death's door. One night he ended up battling a hard-hitting guy who fought like a wrestler. The guy had Mr. I. tackled to the ground, and by all appearances had this fight won. Wrong! Mr. I., in a voice thick with hatred, said, "You have two choices. Either knock me out or kill me because I'm never done." On that last word, Mr. I. jabbed a thumb deep into the guy's eye hoping to blind him. The guy got so freaked out, he jumped to his feet and ran off down the street to escape the crazed opponent who only moments before had been struggling beneath him.

Wilbur was living with Mr. I. and had been having an ongoing problem with three brothers. He was outside of his trailer house when these brothers pulled up in a car looking for a fight with him. Because of his aggressive athleticism, he was able to fight all three at the same time and was doing quite well when suddenly Mr. I. appeared on the steps of the trailer, clad only in underwear and a pair of boots which he'd hastily slipped on upon seeing this mismatched brawl. In a matter of moments, Wilbur and Mr. I. had two of the guys knocked out. The third had escaped by running off down the street and was being pursued by a wild man in underwear. Fear is a great motivator, and Mr. I. soon fell too far behind to continue his pursuit. The two returned to their trailer, going about their business as if nothing had occurred. The defeated duo lying out front eventually came to and drove off.

It was a humid summer night, and Mr. I. was standing by me near the concession stand at the Starlight Drive-In movie theater. He got into an argument with someone he saw who owed him money. "I think I'll kick your scrawny ass," he told the guy, who was small in stature. He grabbed the little guy, spun him around, and booted him twice in the butt.

The little fellow grabbed his backside and sputtered, "I'm going to get Big Bob!" A few minutes later he returned with Big Bob, a strapping man standing 6'3" and weighing 250 pounds.

The man strutted up to Mr. I. and said, "So, you kicked a little guy in the ass? Do you want to try it with me?" Without hesitation or saying so much as one word, Mr. I. unleashed a devastating punch that caught Big Bob right on the nose, nearly knocking him out.

Then he reached down, rolled the big guy onto his stomach, and proceeded to kick him in the butt several times while yelling, "Yes, I will kick you in the ass, too!" He eventually stopped booting the guy and walked back to his car to finish watching the movie. I stood there shaking my head. Big Bob eventually limped off into the night with his scrawny friend, both having learned that you never know when you'll run into someone who is definitely bad to the bone.

Double Murder

Knock, knock, knock. The unexpected sound of knocking on the door usually elicited one of three responses in my head: 1) *Guarded enthusiasm:* Maybe it's a friend dropping by? 2) *Fear:* What's someone doing at the door at this time of the morning? 3) *Annoyance/irritability:* Who's trying to sell me something now?

I opened the door to find two middle-aged men dressed in suits. The gentleman to my right flipped open a wallet at eye level, just like on television, and displayed a gold badge with the police department insignia. My mind quickly started racing through the events of the past few weeks wondering what I'd done to earn a visit from two detectives.

"We're detectives from the Sioux Falls Police Department. Do you own that white pickup parked out front?"

"Yeah, that's my fifty-six Ford pickup," I answered calmly.

"Do you own two dogs, and were you down by Falls Park about two A.M. last night?"

I explained that Curt and I each had a dog, and we were indeed at Falls Park last night letting the dogs go for a swim since it was a hot summer night.

"We need you to come down to the station so we can talk some more."

"Am I under arrest?" I asked, perplexed.

"No, but this is important."

So I went with the detectives to the police station feeling my anxiety increase with each passing block, especially since the detectives rode in complete silence. I wondered why I'd been asked about the dogs. Curt was my roommate and had a German shepherd named Brutus while I had my loyal

115

Doberman, Rebel. I wasn't one to stick around the house much, preferring to be out doing anything as opposed to sitting around. I took Rebel with me everywhere. He was a smart dog that I'd trained to do many tricks, and he'd obediently stay in the back of my pickup whenever I went into a friend's house for an hour or two. He'd never caused any trouble.

The detectives led me into a small interrogation room and sat directly across from me behind a long table.

"Well, I'm going to get right to the point, but first I'll let you know we have your roommate, Curt Ager, in another room talking to other team members of this unit," the shorter detective informed me in a clipped tone. *What the hell is this about?* I wondered. "We have two bodies in the morgue right now, and I'm asking you straight up, were you involved, or was Curt involved in this double murder?"

Whoa! My head spun, and although I knew nothing of this murder I was already thinking of ways to defend myself against the accusation.

"I don't know what you're talking about, but I was not involved in the killing of anybody." I could no longer control my voice, which getting louder and more irritable with the seriousness of what was happening.

"You boys have a past history of violence and arrests, and by your own admission you placed yourself at the crime scene," the taller detective chimed in.

"Look, I told you me and Curt were only swimming our dogs, and that was all we did last night."

The detectives exchanged a brief look. "Are you willing to take a polygraph test?"

At that point, I should have asked to speak with an attorney, but I was convinced that my innocence would be confirmed following this brief lie detector test so I accepted their offer. I was taken to another room where the polygraph examiner attached an arm band similar to a blood-pressure cuff around my bicep, put a sensor around my chest, and sensors on my fingertips. Although innocent, I started to feel sweat forming on my brow so decided it was best to act really relaxed and casual the way an innocent person would. I took slow breaths and tried to answer all their questions as calmly as I could, but I could see the machine dials jumping all over the place and the realization that perhaps I shouldn't have agreed to this crept into my head.

"What is your name? What color are your eyes? Were you at the falls on Saturday night? What's your mother's name? Why were you at the falls? Were you involved in any violent activity Saturday night? What day is it today?"

The questions came as fast as I answered them until suddenly the polygraph examiner stopped and moved me to a room where I waited for what seemed like hours for the results. I paced a little, wondering why the dials had looked so suspicious and why hadn't I asked for a lawyer? My Uncle Allen was a police officer. I should have asked to talk to him. Finally, the door handle rattled and in walked one of the detectives.

"Okay. You're clean and good to go." He drove me back home and on the drive back said that since I'd been run through the mill, he'd call later on and fill me in if he found out anything about the murders. The Bad Santa had passed his polygraph also, but he agreed with me after the fact that we should have asked for legal advice before subjecting ourselves to a polygraph.

The double murder ended up being solved. It turned out that three homeless men down by the falls had all pitched in for a jug of whiskey. They'd been passing the jug around, and one of them thought the other two were gulping down more than their shares. He went into a rage, grabbed a club, and literally beat the other two men's brains out. These murders took place about seventy-five yards from where the Bad Santa and I had been swimming our dogs. The two of us went to find the murder site. There were still blood splatters, skin tissue, and other dried matter that we assumed to be brains as well as human hair on the rocks. The killer was convicted of second-degree murder and sentenced to many years in the South Dakota State Prison.

If I'm ever a murder suspect again, I will definitely lawyer up.

Practicing Medicine Without a License

My buddy Dan emerged from beneath the jacked-up car swearing a blue streak. He'd sliced his arm on some sharp metal while fixing up his car and now blood gushed down from his elbow to his wrist. The two of us examined the deep cut and debated what to do about the injury. It definitely needed stitches.

"Nah, that'd cost too much." So we went inside where he washed the cut with hydrogen peroxide then wrapped the arm with duct tape. When it got infected a few days later, he slathered it with some ointment and long strips of Scotch tape. It healed into a raised, red scar.

When you don't have health insurance, you think twice before seeking professional medical attention. My mom worked an extra job to pay for our insurance when I was in high school, insisting she wouldn't accept any handouts. She associated public assistance with giving up control of your life, a throwback to her childhood days during the Depression when her family was looked down on for being on welfare.

My buddies were usually without insurance and just treated themselves unless hospitalization was vital. It seemed one of us was getting hurt almost every week. We'd all suffered broken bones in our hands from punching people during fistfights. After I left one of my breaks to heal on its own, it developed a bump that remains to this day and now aches with arthritis. Matt broke his hand several times throwing a right hook, once knocking out a guy during a fight over a pool game. I sat on a stool ready to back him up if anyone intervened, but he didn't need my help. After the guy hit the floor cold, his girlfriend came up and tried to attack Matt from behind. She started punching and scratching him, so he squared off and punched her back, knocking out the girl, as well. In the process, he broke his hand and had to go to jail on top of it all. Matt's hand developed a weird shape after numerous untreated breaks.

119

I suffered a broken nose a few times and once decided to set it myself when I was out on my own without insurance. My nose was pushed to the side, so I just took my fist and shoved it back. It bled and made a crackling sound the whole time I was setting it. My nose ended up crooked after this, earning me the name Roman Knuckle Nose from my friends. My sense of smell and taste were never the same after that.

During another barroom brawl, a guy smashed off the end of a beer bottle and used it to stab Matt in the face. The jagged edges caught Matt's upper cheek and the corner of his eye. The eye watered almost nonstop for days, but Matt wouldn't go to a doctor. The injuries eventually healed. During this same altercation, a big guy tackled our buddy, Chuck Kruger, from the side which damaged Chuck's knee. He should have had his knee scoped, but left it untreated and walked with a limp for months.

Jim Anderson, who'd borrowed the cars from the lot for our joy riding, suffered a broken jaw one night while we were fighting. He had to go to the hospital where they wired his jaw shut. Jim quickly tired of being able to drink only what could go through a straw and was constantly complaining about wanting good food. Of course, we responded by tormenting him every time we had pizza or a burger. After only two weeks of having his jaw wired shut, Jim told the Bad Santa to take care of him so he could eat some of our pizza. The Bad Santa got a wire snippers and pliers and cut all the wires holding the jaw shut. Then he used the pliers to pull out all the wires. Jim painfully but happily ate pizza and never did get his jaw rewired.

Another friend of mine suffered a broken hand during a fight over a pool game. He knew he needed medical treatment but had no extra money whatsoever. So, he came up with a scam that required the assistance of the Bad Santa, who worked at a warehouse with this friend where they loaded rolls of carpet into delivery trucks. The following Monday, after an excruciatingly pain-filled weekend, the Bad Santa pretended to have crushed this buddy's hand with the forklift, and the buddy went to the emergency room. Someone from the hospital called back to the business and explained that it not only looked like a three-day-old break, but was also consistent with a break that could be suffered during a fight. The boss told my buddy and the Bad Santa that they could either come clean about how the break happened and just lose their jobs or stick with the story and go to court to face insurance fraud. The next day, they were both looking for new jobs.

So, if someone is going to go out and be a tough guy in the bars, he'd better at least carry medical insurance.

Restless Conscience

I tried with all my might to break the choke hold clamping down on my neck. I was gasping for air, choking for each tiny breath. The hands tightened. It was only a matter of seconds before my esophagus would collapse. *Where's Mr. I.? Where's Matt? I need help, or I'll die!* I struggled and twisted and finally bolted upright in bed, sweating profusely. Another recurring nightmare had invaded my never peaceful mind. This was happening two or three times a week. Even sleep didn't offer rest and tranquility. The dreams were so disturbing that some would stay with me my entire life as if their purposes were so important that the remnants of those tumultuous nights could never be allowed to fade. One nightmare was so realistic that its memory never has escaped my mind. I was fighting with two people and had killed one of them. I could feel the blood running off my hands. The other guy pulled out a pistol. I couldn't run. My legs felt like lead. *Bang!* The handgun went off, and the thud of the hot bullet sliced my back, blasting the life right out of my body.

These violent dreams continued for years and added to the edginess and hostility that dominated my thoughts. I was short-tempered and disagreeable and figured everyone else felt this way, too. So I continued to travel down the same dark roads. For every one good thing that took place, three bad things seemed to overshadow it. My group of friends and I continued to fist fight, commit criminal mischief, and get arrested. We hung out in rough clubs. I bounced around from job to job due to my quick temper that caused persistent issues with bosses and coworkers. I was in a chronic state of anger and irritability. My life passed day by day with no direction.

My Hat's Off to You

Behind me, I heard the pounding of feet on cement and the unwavering shouts from the cop ordering me to stop. *Come on, feet, run faster.* But I wasn't losing this guy, so a few blocks later the cop had closed the distance and he had me. His mission was to put me in cuffs, but I wasn't going to give in willingly. Grabbing me by my coat, the cop tried to put me on the ground. I quickly jumped back and turned on him. With a firm grip on his jacket, I slammed his back into the brick wall of a building. I didn't want to go to jail, plus I was a fighter, and I liked the confrontation at the time. He fought back, but grappling was my specialty, and I put him against the wall again. He'd try to fight back, but into the wall I slammed him a third time. I expected the sound of sirens to start wailing any second and wondered where my buddies were.

It had started off as a good day. I'd won my division in a regional bodybuilding competition. My body was muscular and ripped, and I had even won best abs, beating over twenty other competitors. My friends had all come to watch me compete since one year earlier I'd won the Mr. South Dakota title. When the event was over, it was time to party. Eventually, we ended up in a bar called Fridays in Brookings, South Dakota, to do some more drinking. I had a beer in my hand, and we were all leaving the club to go on to the next bar. Instead of asking me to set my beer down before I walked out, the bouncer at the door decided to use the intimidating approach and jab me with his billy club in my stomach.

"Put the beer on the table," he ordered, scowling and acting cocky, which infuriated me.

Quick as a cat, I snatched the club from his hand.

"Give it back," he demanded in an even louder voice.

"No. You no longer own this billy club, and if you want to stay out of the hospital, don't even think about taking a step toward me," I threatened while handing the club back to the Bad Santa. The bouncer froze, and I could tell he knew I meant business. The Bad Santa, Matt, Leonard Sorenson, and I, all experienced fighters, continued out through the door. Over the pounding music, I could hear the bouncer calling to some other guys to come help him get his billy club.

"Hey, don't call those guys into a situation that you started, and let them end up getting hurt," I yelled back to the bouncer, still completely convinced of our invincibility. He didn't listen, and three of his friends came to his aid. His three friends took a terrible beating while he stood back watching, and we left the trio lying on the street just as a Brookings police car pulled up. It takes a while to beat three guys to the point of being down and out onto the ground, so while this fight raged the police had been called.

I started to walk away, nonchalantly, when the bouncer pointed at me yelling, "Arrest him! He started the whole fight," which led to me being several blocks down the street slamming a cop against a brick wall. I was ready to throw the cop to the ground when I saw Matt, Leonard, and the Bad Santa running down the street toward me. *Wham!* Matt jacked the cop hard and flung him to the sidewalk.

"Don't get up if you know what's good for you," Matt told the cop. The officer didn't move, so we all took off into the night, weaving down empty roads until we'd made it to Leonard's vehicle, which was parked on a dark side street. When we'd all hopped inside the car, Leonard pulled something out from inside his jacket and waved it in the air.

"Look what I've got," he said mischievously, setting the police officer's hat on his head.

"That hat's a great souvenir," I said, roaring with laughter. "Good for you, Leonard."

We made a quick exit from town, feeling pretty superior about outsmarting those small-town authority figures. We drove down the highway with Leonard wearing his new hat like some kind of trophy. None of us noticed the police car in the passing lane which was alongside us. Everything might have been fine if the officer hadn't spotted Leonard's new hat. Red lights were now blinking all around us soon followed by the clang of jail cell doors. We sat behind iron bars waiting to be fingerprinted and booked for numerous charges then escorted to other cells where we spent a fitful night trying to get a restful sleep on a thin jailhouse mattress that was practically useless against the cold steel bed frame.

Clank! Slam! Clank! Slam! There was yelling close by yet it sounded far away. It was the jailers announcing that it was time to get up though we'd barely just fallen asleep. My body ached from fighting and sleeping on a rigid bed. Following a meager breakfast of half an apple, two slices of buttered toast, and a cup of apple juice, another jailer came to our cells.

"You Sioux Falls jailbirds, let's go! Time to talk to the state's attorney."

I was given my street clothes back and changed out of the orange jail jumpsuit I had to put on when we were booked in. My right boot was splattered with blood where I had kicked a guy in the face during our fight in front of Fridays Club. I viewed most people as a problem and a cancer in my life so I had little pity for them. My sense of compassion was dulled to the point where I didn't care if someone got hurt. It was about me, not them, and this blood on my boot illustrated my lack of feelings for others.

We found ourselves sitting behind a mahogany desk in an office lined with bookshelves. I wouldn't realize until many years later how much of an effect the man who was about to enter the room would have on my life. At the moment, I

127

was only concerned about the potential charges that we could be facing and how to find a way out of them.

Soon, a middle-aged man wearing a black suit walked into the office swishing a long, white, red-tipped cane in front of him. I wondered who this man was, perhaps someone to get information from us. Turns out it was the state's attorney, Clyde R. Calhoon. At first, I didn't really hear what he was saying to us, instead focused on wondering how someone who was blind could have ever completed such a high level of college and how he managed to carry out the tasks required of a lawyer. I hadn't known many people with a disability. When I was thirteen years old, I'd worked as a dishwasher at the Driftwood Café along with Thelma, who was intellectually disabled, and Viola, who was deaf. Other than that, people with disabilities were often hidden away. Those with a physical handicap went to the Crippled Children's Home on the other side of town. I had never met a blind person. Mr. Calhoon sat down and got right to the point.

"We're looking at a lot of serious charges here," he said in a stern voice. "I don't know what you boys were thinking last night, but you roughed up a police officer, stole police property, caused a public disturbance, eluded the police, resisted arrest, and one of those young men you beat up in front of Fridays Club ended up in the hospital. Finally, there was quite a bit of marijuana found bagged up under the driver's seat."

It was true. Leonard had brought the bags, intending to make some cash selling the weed to students on campus in that college town. I tallied the charges silently in my head, trying to determine which charges would be felonies. Felonies carry harsh penalties, and there was no one we could pay off this time. The room started closing in on me.

STATE OF SOUTH DAKO ,)
) SS
COUNTY OF BROOKINGS)

IN CIRCUIT COURT
MAGISTRATE DIVISION
THIRD JUDICIAL CIRCUIT

81-2078

STATE OF SOUTH DAKOTA,)
)
Plaintiff,)
)
vs.)
)
PHILIP J. HAMMAN,)
)
Defendant.)

COMPLAINT FOR RESISTING ARREST

VIOLATION OF SDCL 22-11-4

State of South Dakota)
) ss.
County of Brookings)

The undersigned being duly sworn upon oath charges:

That on or about the __22nd__ day of ___February___, 19_81_, in the County of Brookings, State of South Dakota, _____PHILIP J._____ _____HAMMAN_____, did commit the public offense of __Resisting Arrest_____ (SDCL 22-11-4), in that (s)he did then and there intentionally prevent or attempt to prevent a law enforcement officer, to-wit: OFFICER ▓▓▓▓▓▓▓▓▓, acting under color of his authority, from effecting an arrest of said Defendant by threatening to use physical force or violence against said law enforcement officer or using a means which created a substantial risk of causing physical injury to said law enforcement officer and said Defendant did thereby and by said means commit the crime of Resisting Arrest as defined by SDCL 22-11-4;

contrary to statute in such case made and provided against the peace and dignity of the State of South Dakota.

That the complainant states that this Complaint is based upon _personal observation as set forth in the attached Memorandum of Arrest which is true and correct to the best of your complainant's knowledge and information._

Dated this __25th__ day of ___February___, 19__81__ at Brookings, South Dakota.

_____
Complainant

Subscribed and sworn to before me on this __25th__ day of ___February___ 19_81_.

_____
Notary Public - South Dakota

My Commission Expires:
December 22, 1984

REQUEST FOR ARREST WARRANT

CLYDE R. CALHOON, States Attorney in and for Brookings County, South Dakota, hereby requests an Arrest Warrant to be issued based upon the above Complaint.

_____
Brookings County States Attorney

Form 23

129

N⁰ 199111

MEMORANDUM OF ARREST

Name of Person Arrested .... Philip Joseph Hamman .... DOB. 03/07/58

Address .... 615 N. Nesmith Sioux Falls S.D. ....

Offense .... Resisting execution or service of process   22 - 11 - 1 ....

When Arrested ....
Date   Hour

Where Arrested .... On complaint ....

Driver's License 353686-90358 .... Car License .... MNN 3473 .... Make of Car .... Chev ....

Remarks ...... At 12:48 a.m. 02/22/81 the Police Department was notified of a fight at
Friday's. When I got to the scene, ▇▇▇▇▇▇▇ , and employee of Friday's,
stated a person who was walking away (south) had been involved in the fight. I
approached the above mentioned subject and told him I wanted to see an I.D.,
the above mentioned ran. I then proceeded running after the subject and told him
to stop. The subject did stop in front of Rude's furniture. I then again told him
I needed an I.D. We then started to argue and the subject started pushing me. At
this time I was surrounded by 7 or 8 people, these persons pulled the subject
away and surrounded me, pushing me to the ground. These people then ran south.
I returned to the patrol car and started looking for my hat which had been knocked
off during the scuffle. I was travelling south on Main Ave. in the 500 block
when I noticed my hat in the rear deck of a Chevy. I then pulled this car over
and asked for a backup. My hat was then shuffled from the back deck to the front.
I then told the person driving the car to get out. I then identified the driver.
I then asked the next person to get out from the back seat, the above mentioned
subject. The passenger front seat the got out of the car and went towards the
front bumper. The subjects were then handcuffed and my hat was recovered by one
of the subjects from under the car. The above mentioned subject was the transported to the Brookings Police Station at which time I read the subject his
Miranda warning but he stated he was too dumb to understand then. The subject
was then transported to the Brookings County Jail.

District County Judge

Harold's Printing Co.—2M—4-80 166R1

130

STATE OF SOUTH D. KOTA)
) SS
COUNTY OF BROOKINGS)

IN CIRCUIT COURT
MAGISTRATE DIVISION
THIRD JUDICIAL CIRCUIT

81-2084

STATE OF SOUTH DAKOTA,)
)
       Plaintiff,)
)
     vs.)
PHILIP J. HAMMAN,)
LEONARD J. SORENSON,)
MATHEW J. LAFTAN,)
CURTIS L. AGER, Defendants.)

COMPLAINT FOR UNAUTHORIZED
POSSESSION OF MARIJUANA
IN THE SECOND DEGREE

VIOLATION SDCL 22-42-6

State of South Dakota)
) ss.
County of Brookings)

The undersigned being duly sworn upon oath, charges:

That on or about the 22nd day of February , 1981 , in
the County of Brookings, State of South Dakota, PHILIP J. HAMMAN, LEONARD J.
SORENSON, MATHEW J.
LAFTAN, CURTIS L. AGER, did commit the public offense of __Unauthorized

Possession of Marijuana in the (SDCL 22-42-6), in that (s)he did
Second Degree

jointly and knowingly possess a controlled substance, namely, to-wit: Marijuana
in a quantity of more than one ounce but less than one pound, and did thereby commit
the offense of Unauthorized Possession of Marijuana in the Second Degree as defined
by SDCL 22-42-6;

contrary to statute in such case made and provided against the peace and

dignity of the State of South Dakota.

That the complainant states that this Complaint is based upon
personal observation as set forth in the attached Memorandum of Arrest which
is true and correct to the best of your complainant's knowledge and information;

Dated this 25th day of February , 19 81 , at Brookings,
South Dakota.

_____
Complainant

Subscribed and sworn to before me on this 25th day of February,
19 81 .

_____
Notary Public - South Dakota

My Commission Expires:
    December 22, 1984
          REQUEST FOR ARREST WARRANT

CLYDE R. CALHOON, States Attorney in and for Brookings County,
South Dakota, hereby requests an Arrest Warrant to be issued based upon the
above Complaint.

_____
Brookings County States Attorney

Form 21

131

PART THREE

THE
LIGHTED
ROADS

Psalm 119:105

Your word is a lamp unto my feet

and a light unto my path.

Sparks of Light

Through the dark and gloom that cast their long shadows and shielded the light from my life, there were stubborn rays determined to break through. Bill Simon, an easygoing man with a ready smile, was my grade-school basketball coach. He never missed practice, and I soon learned that he was always there for me and the rest of the team. I added him to the short list of people I'd encountered whom I considered dependable. He worked with many kids who came to practice hauling quite a bit of problem baggage along with them, but we all knew Coach Simon cared. He cared enough to hand out genuine encouragement along with doses of reality to push us to be our best.

"Phil, if you want to improve, you must put in extra time beyond our practices," he told me point-blank one night. He could have left for the evening with a quick, "Good job, everyone," but he refused to pacify us with that meaningless platitude. I was starting to revel in being competitive. As soon as I realized I wasn't the best or even at my personal best, I started showing up half an hour early to put in extra time working on my free throws. By the end of the season, I'd earned the ribbon for having the highest free throw percentage. The next year I practiced even harder. At the end of that season, Coach presented me with the same award for the second year in a row. Winning those awards is something I would have never accomplished if he'd accepted my minimal effort.

Freddy was a frail little guy on our team who struggled noticeably with his skills. He couldn't dribble without stumbling on his own feet, and he could barely launch the basketball high enough to make a shot. He'd grimace with all his might and hurl the ball upward where it would swing through the air without coming close to the net. Even so, Coach Simon always found playing time in each game for Freddy, who had yet to score a single shot. Each time Coach put him in the game, everyone held their breath, hoping against hope that this would be the time he would score. Somewhere along the line I adopted the same mindset as Coach regarding Freddy, which was a huge shift for me as I was known for screaming at my teammates and even my best friends when they didn't perform up to par. One time I kicked a teammate who I thought was being lazy during a game we were losing and my mom came out of the stands and pulled me off to yell at me. Coach Simon, the team, and Freddy's parents all sat on pins and needles every time Freddy gained control of the ball and went stumbling down the court where predictably, the ball never fell anywhere near the net.

As the season went on, and we still hadn't seen little Freddy get his two points, hope began to fade. It was nearly the end of the season, and even though he hadn't scored, he never gave up, and Coach commended him for that. It couldn't have been easy for Freddy to watch every other kid hit baskets while he struggled to just get the ball as high as the net. But he didn't quit. I was a starting guard on our team, and during one of the last games Coach had Freddy in with some other players who weren't regular starters. I was sitting on the bench watching the last couple minutes of the game tick by. Someone passed the ball to Freddy, who dribbled a few steps before quickly getting into a determined shooting position. By now, we were no longer holding our breath, having seen miss after miss and realizing that his talents probably were elsewhere. Still, as the few brief seconds passed before he took the shot, the air seemed to quiet. Perhaps like me, the rest of the room was concentrating on willing him to make that basket. Finally, the frail little kid's arms stretched into the air, the ball went sailing, made a slight arc, and *SWISH*, went right into the net! The room came alive with people jumping off their seats yelling, cheering, or pumping their fists in the air. I came off the bench cheering with the others, and when I looked down at Coach Simon, he was jumping up and down. You'd have thought we'd just won the national title. After the game, Freddy's mom stood hugging him over and over, and I knew that someday I wanted to be as fair, encouraging, and dependable as Coach Simon.

****

Judy Jasper was my elementary P.E. teacher, and she pushed me to work beyond my limits for each goal. She didn't let me stop when I set my first goal, the pull-up record, instead encouraging me to go for the push-up record and to improve my running time. Setting records and getting recognition boosted my self-esteem and redirected my energies toward something positive at that time of my life. Years later when I was wrestling on the high school team and on the verge of breaking several school records, I would periodically see her at Washington High events. She continued to remind me that my goals would be reached only by pushing myself *past* my limits. This special woman is someone I will always remember as having influenced my desire to win.

****

Irv Moeller, the tough guy who lived three doors down from me in the Norton section, was a shield from some of my fears in the neighborhood. He lived a hard life and had to overcome a lot, too. When I interviewed him for this memoir, he told me that while growing up he was often bullied by his brother, Donald, as well as others. In turn, Irv came to the defense of others so they wouldn't have to experience what he did. Irv has an unusual nickname. Around town people call him "Happy Birthday." When I called Irv, the first thing he said to me was, "Happy birthday, Phil." When I asked Irv about his nickname, he said this:

"Every day when I wake up, it's like being born again, and I'm thankful to be alive. I had to live through so much, and I've known so many people who died young that every day is a celebration. So, I'm happy you're alive, too, and that's why I'm telling you happy birthday."

137

****

One of the greatest blessings in my life came in the form of aunts and uncles who took me under their wings. They helped with clothes and food knowing what my dad was like and knowing my mom would never ask for help. I often wished I could live with my aunts and uncles because behind closed doors my dad always seemed to find ways to overshadow the good these people brought into my life.

****

I met a friend named Steve Joslyn at a junior high wrestling meet one day. Over the years we faced adversity together, which strengthened our bond. In the Washington High wrestling room, we grappled and bloodied each other during intense practices. Steve was often put into my take-down group even though he was two years younger, and he brawled with us older guys who could unleash violent tempers. Steve always stayed in our wrestling groups, which helped him become a tougher wrestler. I was intense and out of control with my anger while Steve was laid back. Over the years, I learned a lot from his dedication and patience. Most importantly, I never once got arrested or in trouble when I was with Steve. That's proof that the company you're with can affect your decisions. When I was traveling the dark roads of my life, it was Steve who constantly reminded me of things I was doing that were wrong even though I'd get irritated with him for pointing it out. There were times he was able to steer me away from some very dangerous situations, and I've tried to listen to his advice ever since.

****

My teammates during high school wrestling showed me that when we focused together as a group we could accomplish our goals. Together we not only won championships but learned to accept falling short of goals, as well, and to move on. Every one of my varsity wrestling teammates who I stay in touch with went on to be successful in life.

Washington High wrestling coach Ray Wellman was a great inspiration for me. He modeled hard work and dedication. He preached sacrificing for others. "Your wrestling isn't just about you. Your family is watching, your classmates are in the stands, your girlfriends are here, and it's for your teammates and coaches, too. Go out there and give it your all." These words stuck with me my whole life and would echo in my mind to push me to be successful in other aspects. In the spring of my senior year, Coach Wellman asked me, "What are your plans? Are you going to college?"

"I don't think so. Nobody in my family has ever graduated from college."

Coach looked me right in the eyes with the intense gaze which indicated the seriousness of his conviction. He took a step forward. "Yeah, well why not you?"

So I had sparks of goodness here and there. My life, however, lacked an overall philosophy to live by and a path to follow. I had no center. I continued to hang in rough places and make bad choices. Anger, fistfighting, and dangerous activities dominated my world. I couldn't find a way to take the good in my life and put it to productive use. I continued to walk down the same dark roads allowing evil activities to snuff out the sparks.

My grade school basketball coach, Bill Simon.

My grade school PE teacher, Judy Jasper.

My long-time friend, Steve Joslyn.

The intense stare of Coach Ray Wellman (left), and assistant Coach Gary Busch (right).

One of the successful teams I wrestled on in high school. I am standing to the far left. I learned about commitment and hard work from Coaches Wellman and Busch, as well as from my teammates. Due to the school records I set and the many tournaments I won, I was recently inducted into the Washington High School Athletic Hall of Fame, an honor bestowed on only a few other wrestlers.

My Hat's Off to You
[Conclusion]

The state's attorney sat assuredly behind the desk, his face conveying the seriousness of the charges laid out before us. Although his words sounded confident and articulate, the meaning of what he said drifted above me. I'd slept only a few fitful hours, and I couldn't shake the thought from my head that any small hopes I'd had of trying to better my life might be coming to a screeching halt in the next few minutes. For starters, my recent dream of becoming a teacher would be crushed. With a felony, I wouldn't qualify for a teaching license.

"Mr. Lofton, Mr. Sorenson, Mr. Ager, and Mr. Hamman, as well"—I sat attentively upon hearing the state's attorney say my name—"I have the ability to charge each of you with a felony. As it is, I'm placing you boys on probation and fining you for the various charges." With a few more admonishments, he left the room.

Clyde Calhoon was a fair man with an uncanny ability to dole out the appropriate consequences. We'll never know why felonies were not filed. Perhaps in this town, which is home to a large university, he'd seen more than his share of college-aged kids drinking too much and fighting. We waited to be escorted to another room and began a discussion of who might drive the two-hour round trip to haul us back to Sioux Falls since Leonard's car had been impounded. We made several calls, but no one could come to pick us up. We were left with no choice but to call my mom.

She showed up three hours later, irritable, swearing a blue streak, and smoking one cigarette after another. I hopped in the backseat, hoping to avoid talking with my mom the entire drive home. The Bad Santa ended up in the front and made the mistake of putting his feet on the front dash.

"GET YOUR *&%$@# FEET OFF OF THERE! Didn't you ever learn any manners?" she yelled, shoving his feet away. She continued yelling, complaining, and chain smoking the whole way back. Somehow, in all her anger, my mom always had a gleam in her eyes. She seemed to enjoy having a reason to get mad at someone else. For years to come she'd complain about how the Bad Santa had put his feet on her dashboard and shake her head while retelling the story, giving me the feeling she kind of liked revisiting the dysfunctional day when she was the hero who came to Brookings to bring us back home.

While I was in the process of writing this memoir, I called the Brookings, South Dakota, Clerk of Courts to see if they had any record of my arrest and charges. I spoke to an efficient young lady who said she'd search for the records. A couple of days later, I received an envelope with every document I'd been looking for. I called back to thank her.

"By the way, back then you had a visually impaired state's attorney who handled my charges. I'd like to find out if he's still alive and if anyone around there remembers who he is. I'd like to talk to him." I about fell over when she gave me her response.

"The state's attorney you're referring to is Clyde Calhoon, and he's not only still alive, he's still our state's attorney! Mr. Calhoon is in his seventies and has been the state's attorney for over forty years." Here was a man who not only had a strong character, but had served society well for over four decades.

I was able to speak with him and express my long overdue gratitude for making a difference in my life. I asked about his background, and he told me how he'd been in a terrible car wreck that took his sight. Despite this, he went on to graduate from college and law school. When I asked what gave him the drive to overcome blindness, he explained that his parents taught him a strong work ethic from the time he was young and to always make the best out of every situation life hands you. I realized what a great testimony that is to the power of good parenting. My respect for him multiplied. Even in the dark of blindness, light shines through this exemplary man.

When You Stop Chasing the Wrong Thing . . .

Do you believe in destiny? For me, a chance meeting in a parking lot set into motion a chain of events that transformed my life. One cold evening as I was walking into a college hangout to hustle a game of pool, I saw a girl walking to her vehicle which was parked next to mine. I struck up a conversation with her and one thing led to another until I soon found myself dating this pretty, brown-eyed girl named Sandy. We spent time together, went on some dates, and I found for the first time a girl with a love for learning, a love for life, and a strong desire to make the world a better place. What struck me the most was the way her Christ-centered life guided her decisions. She had reasons for what she believed and wasn't easily swayed. This was in stark contrast to the girls I usually dated, girls who lived on the wild side and played hard and fast. Girls who would practically beg to ride on my motorcycle with me. Sandy was adamant about helmets for motorcycle riding. I never wore a helmet. I decided to trick her one day by showing up outside Bergsaker Hall at Augustana College and parking my motorcycle in the circular drive. We were going on a date, and she'd have no choice but to hop on the bike with me even though I had no helmets. I was wrong.

"You don't have a helmet, and you drive too aggressively," she told me. She wasn't prudish about it, she just stuck to her guns. I had to drive across town, drop off my motorcycle, get my pickup, and drive all the way back for our date. Another time I called her from jail in the middle of the night to bail me out.

"You'll just have to stay in jail. I don't have the money to get you out, anyway."

"If you love me, you'd find a way to get the money. I don't want to spend the night here, and I think I need to go to the emergency room for some X-rays."

"I do love you. That's why I'm not bailing you out. All your fighting has to stop." *Click.*

So it was another long, painful night in jail. I was mad about it then, yet for the second time she'd stayed tough. I found myself drawn to this person who set boundaries. Some of my friends thought I should find a different girl. I was torn. After we'd dated a few months, I decided to call my buddy Hal in Venice Beach, California, pack up my pickup truck, and take off thinking I might start over out there. It didn't last long. California was crowded and expensive, two things I disliked. I preferred Sioux Falls where I could find a parking spot right outside my door and order a one-dollar beer at the pool hall.

Something else pulled me back to South Dakota, too. I missed Sandy more than I ever thought I would. She'd been a high school honors student, was on the Dean's List in college, and had friends who were studying to become teachers, nurses, and doctors. What road was I on in life? I began to do some self-reflecting. Sandy came from an upstanding family that loved and supported each other. Her parents invited me to their house for sit-down meals and get-togethers. Yet I knew they had their eyes on me, and rightfully so. Their youngest daughter, at age eighteen, was dating a twenty-four-year-old guy who came from the wrong side of the tracks, wore muscle shirts, had a busted up nose, and was not at all well-mannered. It was a typical good girl–bad boy situation. Sandy asked her mom what she thought of me after we'd dated a short time.

"He has a lot of tattoos," her mom responded politely. Who knows how many sleepless nights Sandy's parents spent worrying about their baby girl. There's an old saying that behind every good man there's a good woman. In our case, Sandy was a good woman behind not such a good man. I was still running with a rough crowd and getting into trouble, yet I started to notice a change in myself. Sandy's patience with me was wearing thin, but she invited me to church and gave me a Bible to study, which I did. I was extremely skeptical, though. I was primarily scouring the Bible looking for contradictions and errors but had yet to find one.

During the sermons, it felt like the pastor was speaking directly to me. *Yes, I felt lost. Yes, I was a bitter person who sought revenge. No, I did not have pity on others, and I surely did not forgive anyone.* The words that flowed from the pulpit softened my heart and opened my mind to a new philosophy regarding life about which Christ spoke.

I continued to study. Being an expert at finding loopholes, I tried to find flaws in what Christ said. I still couldn't find any. I started to think that perhaps I'd found The Truth. Truth was important to me since I had grown up distrusting people. There were historical predictions that Jesus could not have manipulated. Events were foretold many years before Christ was born such as where he'd be born, how he'd be received by the people, how he'd die, and for what reason. The truth finally hit me harder than I'd ever been hit in a street fight.

It is said that the Old Testament is the New Testament concealed and the New Testament is the Old Testament revealed. The more I learned, the more I changed. The violence that had been raging inside of me for years started to mellow, making room for peace I'd never imagined could exist within me. Sleep came easy now, and the bad dreams that had plagued me for years just disappeared and never returned. I started spending less time with rough people in rough places. The fistfighting stopped. Was I perfect? Not by a long shot. I am still human and have to stay focused to walk the lighted roads. So I set new goals in my life and made the changes I needed in order to reach them.

There had been other changes in my life, too. After my dad had taken off with one of his other women, my mom grew more bitter. I had a hard time distancing myself from some of my friends who were like brothers to me, but we weren't good for each other. My friends went off and had to find their own way in life. But there were more happy changes than sad ones.

Sandy and I were married. A few years later my life seemed almost perfect after our son, Jordan, and daughter, Angela, had arrived to fill our house with more love. When you stop chasing the wrong things, the right things have a chance to catch you. I am a different person today, and I was guided here by Sandy's love and changed by the love of Christ. To me, it is proof of the power of Christ.

New Fear

'Twas grace that taught my heart to fear, and grace my fears relieved. These lines from the powerful song, "Amazing Grace," made me think of how I'd handled my fears in the past, through my own bloody hands and fighting. With Christ in my life, I had a new fear, the fear of a wasted life.

I developed a new outlook for my future focusing on how I could make a difference in the world. God gives us all different talents so we can reach out to others and make their lives better. I began to think of where my talents might lie. I was a good athlete and good with kids as well as being good in confrontational situations. So when one of my college professors suggested that perhaps I was cut out for working with students with behavior disorders, I knew that would be one of my purposes in life in addition to coaching. I completed a special education degree and did graduate work in the area of behavior disorders. My life now had a center and a philosophy to live by. For the past thirty years now I've worked with high school students with behavior disabilities, a job that has a burnout rate of five years. This is where God led me.

Sandy and I are dressed up for a fundraiser.

We have been married since 1984.

Sacrifice

The wrestling meet had come down to the final match, a clash between the two heavyweight wrestlers. The crowd was going wild. People were on their feet stomping on the wooden bleachers and yelling until the noise grew deafening. We were the visiting team at Bishop Heelan High School. The scoreboard had just lit up with the new tally: Visitors – 31, Home – 32. This dual meant more to me than just about any meet we'd faced in the five seasons I'd been head coach at Sioux City East High. We had yet to beat our cross-town rival, Bishop Heelan. In fact, no team in the city had beaten them in almost a decade. They had a stranglehold on the city and dominated wrestling in an area that prides itself on producing some of the finest grapplers in the nation.

By now, our varsity wrestlers had risen to their feet cheering, and students were coming out of the bleachers en masse to be there when our heavyweight wrestler, David Lee Rice, stepped on the mat. Our assistant coach, Vince, was at a meet with the JV squad. Vince, weighing in at nearly 300 pounds, was a no-nonsense former wrestler and veritable tough guy himself who wrestled with David almost daily in the practice room and knew him well since Vince was the heavyweight coach. So tonight, David only had me rather than Vince, who was usually right in David's face, nose-to-nose, barking at him before every match. As a ninth grader, David had been quick and athletic but lacked confidence and mental toughness. By now, we'd grown to depend on him in a clinch as many team wins fell on his shoulders since the heavyweights were always the last to wrestle at that time. Sweat was dripping down both of his cheeks, but his face revealed a firm resolve.

When he walked by me heading to the mat, I said these few words: "Remember, David, sacrifice."

I often told our team that wrestling was not just about them but was for many others, too. "Those matches are for your parents, the fans, your teammates, classmates, and our school's reputation. Work hard and make the sacrifice for others." These were the same words my high school coach had told me, and these words had served me well in my life.

The six-minute match was a white-knuckler. It was a close match the whole way. In the last seconds, David stayed in control, but there was time for his opponent to score and win. When the buzzer went off, David had won! A roar exploded from the crowd. The referee raised David's hand, and as he walked toward our bench grinning, the team swarmed him. That victory set our team on the road to wrestling domination in the city at that time. From that point on, we started beating our rival on a regular basis.

David had made the sacrifice for his team. I could not have felt more proud of him. He left the gym a hero.

David enlisted in the U.S. Army and left for boot camp after graduation in 2001. Four years later he was on his second tour and stationed in Iraq. The soldiers stationed with him grew to appreciate his fun-loving humor and work ethic. He did everything in his typical big way. As a child, he didn't have a few G.I. Joes, he had tubs full of them. As a teenager, he accumulated over 600 DVDs and CDs. As a soldier, he gave it his all, becoming a fire support specialist as well as a role model to others and loved serving his country.

One day I happened to be in the school office when David's mom showed up accompanied by two solemn military officials. They'd all come as quickly as they could. With the increasing popularity of cell phones and texting at the time, word could spread quickly and they wanted to pull his sister, Stevie, out of class to give her the news before she heard it from someone else. A rocket-propelled grenade had struck David's vehicle causing it to roll, and he didn't make it out alive. A sickening pall spread through the office and then the school.

After his funeral, the streets of our city were lined for miles with hundreds of people of all ages who stood along the funeral route waving American flags or standing with their hands over their hearts. It was a moving tribute of patriotism for a fallen soldier.

David had made the ultimate sacrifice for his country. I could not have felt more proud of him. He left this world a hero.

Truth and Consequences

I hear a lot of tough talk that just doesn't cut it with me. *I don't need anybody because I make my own way in life. I don't care what anyone thinks because I do what I want when I want. If other people don't like it, they can go to* *&%#. You get the drift, people who are so strong that they don't care if the world is against them. I don't buy it. Maybe it's because I used to feel the same way, but now I know there's a softer road to choose. Or maybe it's because I *still* feel the same way but to a lesser degree. I do know there are consequences to every action and those consequences can be good or bad.

I now know that it's okay to tell people I won't put up with their crap and then beat the tar out of them, as long as I'm okay with having a warrant out for my arrest, paying fines, getting probation, and hearing a cell door slam behind me.

It's all fun and good to go where I want when I want and to frequent shady places with shady people and have a great time doing it because I'm only going to live once, even though I may not live long if someone pulls a weapon on me and puts my life on the line.

I learned from my dad that it's okay to abuse or degrade your kids because you can always use that sorry excuse about how you're just toughening them up. And this is especially not a problem if you want to grow old alone and confused, wondering why your kids and family don't want anything to do with you.

I've learned that only thinking about myself is what makes me wake up empty and unfulfilled. If I want satisfaction in life, it requires effort. It requires using the gifts and talents I've been given to make the world a better place.

I've learned that I can go ahead and hate my neighbor or turn my back on my family instead of mending fences. If there's a problem, I can just keep it going so I don't look like I've given in. But if I want peace of mind and to sleep

157

well at night I need to make the first move toward forgiveness and to surround myself with the strength of a church family.

I know that when life gets busy, with long work hours and stressful deadlines, that I can't sacrifice quality time with my family. Nothing is more important than maintaining some sit-down meals, helping the kids with homework, attending their events, getting to know their friends, and listening to what is going on in their lives. I can't say that family is the most important thing in my life without doing those things.

Forgiveness can be difficult. I had a hard time forgiving my dad for damaging me as well as other family members. I have forgiven him, yet there are times when a particularly bad memory will worm its way back into my soul. When that happens, I have to remind myself that it's in God's hands now. I can elect to walk on His peaceful path or become consumed with anger and spitefulness.

I've learned that healthy relationships require conversation, compromise, and compliments. Kind words are the catalyst that bonds a family. Love is the best thing we can give.

We get only one chance on this earth to make a difference. We all affect others in a positive or negative way through what we do or what we fail to do. Everyone has gifts. Sometimes we take our gifts and talents for granted, and that can only lead to one thing: a wasted life. It took me a long, long time to sort through a lot of twisted garbage that had been planted in my mind, but the hard changes I made were worth it. I can only hope that by baring my mistakes to the world, others might decide a different path, and I can save them some heartache. If young people are mature enough to be reading this book, they're mature enough to start putting their own feet onto the lighted roads. All a person has to do is ask a school counselor, teacher, pastor, or coach because it's no secret that any one of them would be honored to be part of helping to steer someone in the right direction. Finally, we should sacrifice a little time each day to give thanks to The One who's sacrificed so much for us. Because of Him, I now have my life in order instead of living in disorder.

19448481R00095

Made in the USA
Middletown, DE
21 April 2015